PEACE CATALYSTS

Resolving Conflict in Our Families, Organizations and Communities

RICK LOVE

IVP Books
An imprint of InterVarsity Press
Downers Grove, Illinois

InterVarsity Press
P.O. Box 1400, Downers Grove, IL 60515-1426
World Wide Web: www.ivpress.com
Email: email@ivpress.com

InterVarsity Press® is the book-publishing division of InterVarsity Christian Fellowship/USA®, a movement of students and faculty active on campus at hundreds of universities, colleges and schools of nursing in the United States of America, and a member movement of the International Fellowship of Evangelical Students. For information about local and regional activities, write Public Relations Dept., InterVarsity Christian Fellowship/USA, 6400 Schroeder Rd., P.O. Box 7895, Madison, WI 53707-7895, or visit the IVCF website at www.intervarsity.org.

While all stories in this book are true, some names and identifying information in this book have been changed to protect the privacy of the individuals involved.

Cover design: Cindy Kiple
Interior design: Beth Hagenberg
Images: © frentusha/iStockphoto

ISBN 978-0-8308-3668-0 (print)
ISBN 978-0-8308-9632-5 (digital)

Printed in the United States of America ∞

InterVarsity Press is committed to protecting the environment and to the responsible use of natural resources. As a member of Green Press Initiative we use recycled paper whenever possible. To learn more about the Green Press Initiative, visit www.greenpressinitiative.org.

Library of Congress Cataloging-in-Publication Data

A catalog record for this book is available from the Library of Congress.

P 18 17 16 15 14 13 12 11 10 9 8 7 6 5 4 3 2 1
Y 29 28 27 26 25 24 23 22 21 20 19 18 17 16 15 14

"This fascinating book provides a refreshing call to arms for Christians and non-Christians alike to think deeply and seriously about becoming peacemakers. Through a masterful blend of Scripture and personal experience, Rick Love makes a compelling case for why each of us should seek to live out the kind of peace that Jesus modeled for believers of every stripe, the 'peace that transcends all understanding.'"

Douglas M. Johnston, president and founder, International Center for Religion & Diplomacy

"As conflicts around the world continue to escalate, Christian peacemakers have an unparalleled opportunity to be true ambassadors of reconciliation. This book gives a long-overdue call to the church to embrace the call to be peacemakers in all areas of life while giving concrete lessons on how to do it."

Lisa Gibson, global conflict coach and author of *Releasing the Chains* and *Life in Death*

"This book is an urgent call to join the journey of peace with Jesus. Rick's personal storytelling approach embodies the old adage 'peace begins with me.' By citing both beautiful and painful personal examples of forgiveness and reconciliation, he draws us into the story of how God is at work today making peace between traditional 'enemies.' There is enduring wisdom here as well as a caution about going it alone: 'Peacemaking is a community discipline.' This story of God's invitation to wholeness, plenitude and peace—shalom—should become our story. There are no shortcuts to peace, it is the work of justice. To get started, Rick equips the reader with eight practical peacemaking steps that anyone can begin to take today. Let us pray that this book begins a robust evangelical conversation about peace at home and around the world."

Matthew Scott, director of peacebuilding, World Vision International

"*Peace Catalysts* compellingly integrates evangelical witness with peacemaking commitment. Fascinating anecdotes with practical guidance for peacemakers make lively reading. This book is Christ centered and biblically grounded. Rick Love describes with surprising candor the personal challenges of serving Christ as a peacemaking emissary. Those committed to local and global mission will find this book to be a necessary resource in these tumultuous times."

David W. Shenk, global consultant for Christian/Muslim relations, Eastern Mennonite Missions

"As pastor of a large church and as a leader who oversees other churches, I found Rick Love's material on conflict resolution to be the most practical, irenic and helpful material I have ever read on this subject. *Peace Catalysts* is engagingly written and obviously springs from Love's vast experience in leading teams and organizations in a variety of international and local settings. *Peace Catalysts* is a book for this exact moment in history—a time of partisan rancor and polemical pundits. I love this book and pray that it would get into the hands of every Christian leader."

Rich Nathan, senior pastor, Vineyard Columbus, author of *Empowered Evangelicals* and *Both-And*

"We wish for it, talk about it, even pray that God will bring it, but few of us really understand the meaning of peace. That's why *Peace Catalysts* is such an important book. In a straightforward and clear style, Rick Love discusses the theological and practical implications of peace and through stories and examples shows us how to become catalysts for it in our homes and communities. Never shying away from the tough questions, he offers sound wisdom and helpful tools to use for both preventing conflicts and resolving them. This book is an excellent resource for both individuals and groups, and will certainly become a classic."

Dale Hanson Bourke, author of *The Israeli-Palestinian Conflict: Tough Questions, Direct Answers*

"Rick Love has masterfully crafted a text that speaks to peace, a much-neglected issue despite the fact that conflict and lack of harmony are so universal. So in this sense, he has written a book that everybody needs but perhaps does not know they need! Rick Love speaks authoritatively because his wisdom is borne out of personal experience. Biblically sound and interwoven with real, powerful stories, this peacemaking guide will simultaneously open your eyes to the problem and provide helpful solutions."

Allen Yeh, associate professor of intercultural studies and missiology, Biola University; founder and chairman of the world Christianity consultation at the Evangelical Theological Society

"All Christians—from pacifists to just war advocates and everyone in between—should read *Peace Catalysts* since we can all do better at resolving conflicts. Rick Love's book descends from the abstract level of theory to empower and equip peacemakers. Our families, organizations and communities will be glad that we've read this book!"

Amos Yong, J. Rodman Williams Professor of Theology and dean, Regent University School of Divinity, Virginia Beach, Virginia

"For years I read about 'the God of peace' and 'the peace of God.' For years I prayed that 'the peace of Christ' might dwell within me, and I celebrated the birth of 'the Prince of peace.' Then I started visiting war zones: first Bosnia, later the Democratic Republic of Congo, now the Holy Land. Peace is no longer a pretty notion somehow associated with divine beings. People I meet are dying for peace, literally. This book provides practical guides for helping to create personal peace, interpersonal peace, social peace and peace as an alternative to war. In my life and ministry, I need this book!"

Lynne Hybels, advocate for global engagement, Willow Creek Community Church

"I couldn't put this book down. It's brilliant and simple at the same time. It is the most practical thing I've seen for being a peacemaker in everyday life for everyday disciples ever. Whether you have a conflict in your family or you're working globally dealing with conflicts, this book is a must-read."

Bob Roberts Jr., senior pastor, NorthWood Church, author of *Bold as Love*

CONTENTS

1

GOT CONFLICT?

Love is the only force capable of transforming an enemy into a friend.
We get rid of an enemy by getting rid of enmity.

MARTIN LUTHER KING JR.

FOLLOWING THE PRINCE OF PEACE INTO A WORLD OF CONFLICT

The word *peace* conjures up different things for different people. I am a child of the sixties, so my generation links peace with hippies, anti-Vietnam war protests and free love. Others think of beauty queens declaring their hope for world peace. (I can't help but picture Sandra Bullock in *Miss Congeniality.*) Many conservative evangelicals assume peace is for liberals, whether theological or political. Other evangelicals, who appreciate the Bible's emphasis on peace, tend to have a narrow view of God's peace purposes, focusing primarily on interpersonal peacemaking among believers. Peace for them is often unrelated to the gospel, the kingdom of God or the pressing social issues of the day. No wonder so many evangelicals feel that the concept of peace is wimpy.

But is peace only relevant for the faithful few? Is peace just for hippies, beauty queens and liberals?

Jesus didn't think so. Peace is a major piece of the Bible. It's *big*. One of Jesus' most prized titles is Prince of Peace (Isaiah 9:6). This One who invites all people to follow him is the source of peace in a world of conflict. And Jesus knows his stuff. We do well to obey what he says about conflict resolution.

This book started as a primer and was going to be short. But I kept writing. In this book, I outline the *how to* of Jesus' teaching on peacemaking. But my greater desire is to inspire you to *want to* be a peacemaker. I have written this to help you follow the Prince of Peace. He will help you resolve your conflicts and become a peace catalyst.

THE PAIN OF CONFLICT

Conflict is a painful fact of life. Many of us have not experienced the trauma of war or the violence of racism, but we have all been wounded by words. We have felt both the discomfort and the distress of discord. And we know that, sadly, unresolved conflict poisons relationships and multiplies alienation (Hebrews 12:14-15).

The first recorded conflict in Scripture took place in a family. No surprises here. The family should be a place of comfort, safety and support, but it often becomes a battleground. That's what happened between Cain and Abel (Genesis 4:1-16). Cain was jealous of his brother because God accepted Abel's offerings and rejected his. So Cain became angry and brutally murdered Abel.[1]

Few of us have experienced such violence in our families, but we all know family pain and brokenness at some level. Sometimes it comes from parents; other times it comes from our siblings or even our extended family. Verbal jabs and mean-spirited putdowns scar our psyche. The very people who should love us don't have time for us. The people who should be eager to hear about our successes or bear our burdens don't always seem to care. We feel forced to live up to parental expectations or dreams that don't fit our gifting or natural bent.

My friend Robert stood outside my parents' house talking with his wife, Betty, who had been driving by and stopped to talk. I was happy to see this, because they had been having struggles in their marriage. But the conversation soon got heated and escalated into a shouting match. Betty peeled out in her car—tires squealing. Robert ran down the driveway in rage. He screamed and hit the garage door, nearly breaking his hand. This big, strong man wept in my arms as I tried to comfort and calm him. Months later they divorced.

We also experience conflict in our organizations. Without a doubt, the most painful and prolonged conflict I ever experienced was when I became the CEO of the US branch of the faith-based organization Frontiers in 1993. I got caught between Frontiers' international board of directors and its US board. The international board had decided they wanted a new, visionary leader to head up their US office. They unanimously and unilaterally wanted to install me as the new CEO.

The US board perceived my appointment as a power play. They felt the international board had not treated them as equal partners. So the US board firmly rejected me. And I felt the brunt of these opposing entities. The relationship between the two boards remained in an ugly stalemate for months. Finally, the entire US board resigned from Frontiers.

What an auspicious start! I was the CEO of an organization whose whole board had just quit. I not only had to endure the stinging criticisms and rejection of the US board, but I also had to face public shame, as *Christianity Today* covered the story. The first mention of my name in print as a Christian leader was surrounded by controversy. Not what I had hoped for.

Not only this, but I inherited a group of thirty dedicated and gifted staff members who didn't want me to be their leader. I had been forced on them. They had had no part in the process, no say in my appointment. They too were in pain. Although I was distressed, I felt worse for them. One woman leader said the transition felt like emotional rape. Others didn't use such strong language to describe their feelings, but they were hurt. In one meeting I actually got an intense side ache as I listened to them talk about their distress over the transition.

My first day in the office as CEO was not pretty. I interviewed every person. I asked them about their jobs, entreated them to give me a chance and promised to become a leader they could trust. The first few months were intense. In some ways, I was the enemy, and at times I felt some of them were my enemy. So, much of my time was spent working for peace. I repeatedly and humbly confessed that the leadership transition was a disaster and that I was sorry it had happened.

Empathetic listening to others' pain proved to be one key to making peace at Frontiers. I focused on loving the team and trying to keep them focused on our mandate as an organization. As you can imagine, the first few months were rocky. I came home at the end of every day emotionally drained. But little by little, relationships healed, and my leadership was accepted.

During the most heated moments of the conflict, the wisest, most levelheaded person on the original US board took me aside and said, "Rick, I think the most important thing you can learn from this conflict is the importance of processing decisions. You need to listen to and understand both sides." He was right. That was a huge lesson. I didn't realize it then, but God was teaching me about conflict and mediation. We could have used some wise, trusted mediators to help us navigate our differences.

It is often said that there are at least two sides to every issue. This transition taught me to be sensitive to all sides. God used the pain of this conflict to help shape me into a peacemaker. This experience also helped form my definition of peacemaking: "resolving conflict and restoring harmony."

THE RELUCTANT PEACEMAKER

I did not choose to be a peacemaker; it chose me. I was busy minding my own business, trying to follow Jesus and change the world. But I found myself surrounded by conflict. Often the conflict was collateral damage from my own zealous attempts to turn the world upside down for Christ. Though that's humbling to admit, it's true. And occasionally the conflict was caused by others. But either way, I found myself in the middle of it. And though I didn't appreciate it at the time, the Prince of Peace was leading me.

It was disappointing to realize that I was not yet equipped for a role as a peacemaker. I had studied at two well-respected schools in the United States, Westminster Theological Seminary and Fuller Theological Seminary. But no one at either school had taught me about the peaceable ways of Jesus. I had to learn the hard way. Conflict would ambush me—with a vengeance.

It had begun long before with a church split at the church where I was a pastor. Since I was planning to move to Indonesia to be a missionary, I had been mentoring a gifted man to take over my role at the church. We had a strong difference of opinion about how we should fulfill the Great Commission. Such a strong difference of opinion, in fact, that it led to a church split. Wonderful. If I had been as committed to the Great Commandments (love of God and neighbor) back then as I was the Great Commission, things may have been different.

Once I arrived in Indonesia, the ministry teams I led also experienced conflict. (I'm happy to say it was not always because of me.) One conflict in particular stands out because it was so surprising. I welcomed a couple to our team who were close friends with one of our veteran couples. I thought their presence would enhance team dynamics for sure. But only a short time later, I ended up doing shuttle diplomacy, driving back and forth between their houses, relaying their messages to one another. They had intense differences of opinion over their approach to ministry and lifestyle that hadn't been evident during their friendship in the United States. We learned that culture shock not only throws off people's equilibrium, it also heightens conflict. And again I was in the middle of it. So I began learning how to mediate conflict.

Living, working and doing doctoral study in Indonesia provided another eye-opening experience. The Sundanese (the second most populous ethnic group in Indonesia) struggled with right relationships. They were polite on the outside but held grudges on the inside.

Again I was forced to be a peacemaker.

Here's an example. One day a young married couple stopped by to talk, so I took them into my office. Paul and Linda had been following Jesus for a short time and, like everyone, had brought a lot of baggage into their marriage. The minute we sat down, Paul blurted out, "I wanna get a divorce!" With a pained look on his face, he described his hurt and his reasons for wanting a divorce. He said he couldn't trust Linda because of her past relations with men. And Linda said she couldn't respect Paul because he was lazy. Hurt spilled over from both sides.

I am not a marriage counselor, but I knew enough to actively listen. Then I looked them in the eye and said with all the authority I could muster, "No, you are not getting a divorce!"

However, the accusations continued to push and pull the conflict back and forth. I spent more than two hours calming them down and challenging them to make peace. I urged them to take responsibility for their own issues, to get the logs out of their own eyes before they dealt with their spouse's issues. I pleaded with them to trust and obey Jesus. I repeatedly challenged them to love and forgive one another.

After those two hours of the "blame game," they grew weary of the fight. My admonitions began to sink in, and Paul's heart softened. He confessed that he shouldn't judge Linda because of her past. He said he needed to forgive her and love her for who she was at that moment. Linda responded to his conciliatory gesture and asked for forgiveness too. We had a tearful and joyful time of reconciliation.

This was a watershed event in their marriage. But reconciliation is a journey, not an achievement. So Paul and Linda needed ongoing encouragement. My wife and I continued to help them work toward oneness in their relationship. I am thrilled to say that they remain happily married (realizing that even healthy marriages have rocky moments).

Personal experiences of conflict like this weren't the only things shaping me as a reluctant peacemaker. More than a decade later, the evil of terrorism crashed into my life. Like much of the rest of the world, I sat stunned before the television as I watched the devastating terrorist attacks of September 11, 2001, play over and over and over again. Like most Americans, I felt numb and angry.

And, as we all know, tensions between Muslims and the West soared after that. Most Christians in the West quickly mimicked their unbelieving neighbors, believing that all Muslims—not just a few evil extremists—were the enemy. The events surrounding 9/11 pushed me further into peacemaking. My focus until 9/11 had been interpersonal peacemaking, but I now felt like God was leading me to address broader social dimensions as well.

So I stepped down from my role as Frontiers' international director (a role I'd been in since 2000) and went on a sabbatical. I was accepted into the Yale Center for Faith and Culture's Reconciliation Program as a post-doctoral fellow. I looked forward to a time of writing and reflection as I transitioned into the role of peacemaker. But my time at Yale was anything but reflective.

On October 13, 2007, 138 influential Muslim clerics, representing every school and sect of Islam from around the world, wrote an open letter to Christians everywhere, calling for dialogue based on the common ground of "love of God and neighbor." This open letter was called "A Common Word."[2] The most famous response to this call for dialogue was issued by the Reconciliation Program, which in turn resulted in a global conference at Yale University on July 24–31, 2008.

The leaders of the Yale Center for Faith and Culture asked me to help them put on the conference at Yale. So instead of simply studying about peacemaking, I got a chance to learn practically about it during my sabbatical. I did some research, but most of my time was spent preparing for and putting on the Common Word Conference.[3]

Seventy-five high-level Muslim leaders joined seventy-five high-level Christian leaders for a week of dialogue about the Great Commandments. This unprecedented global conference was a turning point in my life. I have never met so many Muslim scholars, sheikhs, grand muftis and princes. More importantly, learning about Islam directly from these Muslim leaders and getting to know them personally over meals impacted me profoundly. I began to devote myself to becoming a full-time peacemaker and to breaking down barriers between Christians and Muslims. God was calling me to be a bridge builder.

Think about this: Christians and Muslims comprise over half the world's population (see figure 1.1). If we can't have peace between Christians and Muslims, then it will be virtually impossible to have peace in the world. As I continued to ponder and pray, I sensed God calling me to start Peace Catalyst International, the nonprofit organization I currently lead.

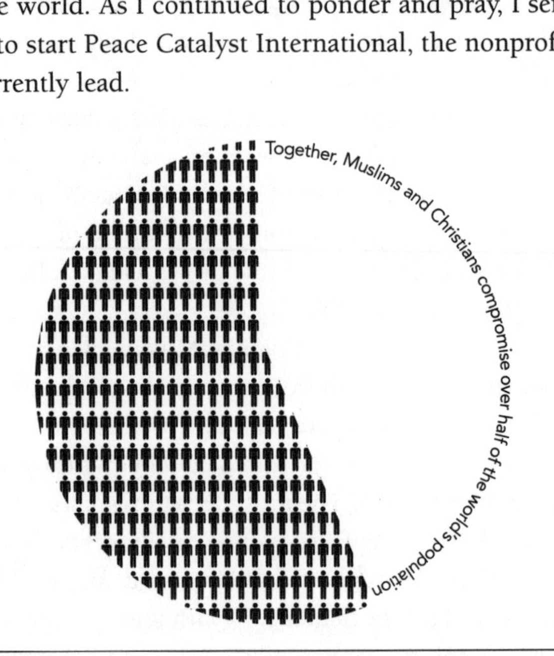

Figure 1.1

On the way to changing the world, the Lord changed me. Everywhere I turned, people held grudges, harbored hurt feelings and experienced broken relationships. Once I began making peacemaking a major theme of my life, a good friend and coworker said to me, "It must be great to be known as a peacemaker."

"Well," I said, "peacemaking is no fun. It's really hard. But I do it because this is what Jesus taught. Peacemaking is a commitment to obey Christ's commands regarding relationships. Peacemaking is love in action."

I am a reluctant peacemaker. You might be too. Welcome to the journey!

PEACEMAKING FOR DUMMIES

A One-Verse Peacemaking Manual

If I had to choose only one verse in the entire Bible to summarize what Jesus expects of peacemakers, it would be Romans 12:18. It's concise and comprehensive—perfect for peacemaking dummies like me: "If it is possible, as far as it depends on you, live at peace with everyone."

Notice how realistic Paul was about waging peace. The condition "if it is possible" acknowledges that it is not always possible to make peace. Scripture is realistic about conflict and discord. Biblical peacemaking is neither sentimental nor naive. It addresses the harsh realities of brokenness and evil. (Check out the entire passage—Romans 12:17-21—to understand the full context of this important verse.) Even our most sincere efforts may fail. *Peacemakers aren't always peace achievers.*

This verse also affirms proactive peacemaking: "If it is possible, as far as it depends on you . . ." Since making peace involves at least two parties, reconciliation isn't always possible. But the responsibility for taking steps toward peace always rests on us as individuals. We can't ignore it, and we can't wait for the other party to come to us. We are repeatedly commanded to take the initiative in pursuing peace ourselves.

These additional verses drive home the same truth:

> Therefore, if you are offering your gift at the altar and there remember that your brother or sister has something against you, leave your gift there in front of the altar. First go and be reconciled to that person; then come and offer your gift. Settle matters quickly with your adversary who is taking you to court. Do it

> while you are still together on the way, or your adversary may hand you over to the judge, and the judge may hand you over to the officer, and you may be thrown into prison. Truly I tell you, you will not get out until you have paid the last penny. (Matthew 5:23-26)

> If a brother or sister sins, go and point out the fault, just between the two of you. If they listen to you, you have won them over. (Matthew 18:15)

> So watch yourselves. If a brother or sister sins against you, rebuke them; and if they repent, forgive them. (Luke 17:3)

> Make every effort to live in peace with everyone and to be holy; without holiness no one will see the Lord. (Hebrews 12:14)

Finally, notice the last phrase of Romans 12:18: "live at peace with everyone." The Bible teaches peacemaking without borders. The pursuit of peace knows no barriers. The scope of peacemaking is comprehensive. God expects us to pursue peace with family, friends, neighbors, atheists, Muslims, undocumented immigrants, gays, Democrats and Republicans.

God's peacemaking plan is comprehensive. Peacemaking pushes us beyond our comfort zone and outside the walls of our churches. It challenges us to live out the peaceable ways of Jesus with our neighbors and our enemies. No borders. No boundaries. No exceptions.

During a Vineyard conference, Pastor Randy Sutter walked up to me and said, "Rick, I read your book on peacemaking and it doesn't work!"[4] I smiled and asked him, "What do you mean?" He proceeded to tell a gut-wrenching story of betrayal, a pastor's worst nightmare—except it really happened.

"I went on a sabbatical—my first and only one in nineteen years of ministry," he said. "The first two and a half months went well. But then I heard about trouble brewing in our church. Seven staff members had decided they wanted to get rid of Alice and me and bring in a new pastor. All hell broke loose. When we finally returned, we had lost our staff and about 250 church members."

I groaned and said, "So sorry to hear that. Please tell me how it happened."

"Well, Rick, the staff members leading this coup spread lies and false accusations about us for months before we heard anything. When we got word of this plot against us, we got counselors and our overseers in the Vineyard involved in helping us work through the conflict. The staff gave the counselor a list of forty-two accusations against us. But the investigation concluded that all the accusations were false. There had been no pastoral misconduct by either me or Alice. Of course, we were happy about the results of the investigation. But our critics refused to meet with us individually. They were not willing to reconcile, and the church remained split."

"I can't imagine the pain you experienced," I said. "So then what happened?"

"Early on I heard the Lord tell me to own your own sins, whether they were real or perceived, intentional or unintentional, and ask for forgiveness and get out of the way. So Alice and I concentrated on modeling and teaching about forgiveness for the first year back with the church."

Randy and Alice are my heroes. They worked hard at getting the plank out of their own eye (Matthew 7:3-5); they forgave those who sinned against them; and they loved their enemies. They experienced one of the worst kinds of betrayal and through forgiveness were able to emerge as models for their church and for all of us.

Yes, peacemakers aren't always peace achievers. Numerous factors hinder the church from being a reconciling community. Because of this, I want to make one important observation about this excruciating church split: peacemaking often fails because there are too few leaders in the local church equipped and committed to making peace. It is not enough to have one or two leaders modeling unswerving obedience to the peaceable ways of Jesus. It takes a group of equipped peacemakers to protect the community against the inimical, divisive work of a few.

It may help to visualize an intense conflict like this as if it were a raging fire. Peacemakers are firefighters who pour water on the flames. The problem is that peace breakers pour gasoline on the same fire. It takes lots of water to put out a relational fire like that.

As a young pastor, I got embroiled in a painful conflict that resulted in a church split. Like Randy, I was the one being accused. Two of the other pastors weighed into the fray, working hard at resolving the conflict. But to no avail. They lacked a supporting cast; there were no other peacemaking leaders standing with them. Eventually I was absolved and proven to be in the right. But that's hardly gratifying, because the community was fractured and everyone was hurt.

I am not saying Randy and Alice's church wouldn't have split if they had enough leaders trained in peacemaking. But I am saying that one reason peacemakers aren't peace achievers is because too few members of the church have the knowledge and skills to respond to conflict as Jesus commands. Peacemaking is a community discipline.

2

WHAT PEACE CATALYSTS BELIEVE

God is a peace-loving God and a peacemaking God. The whole history of redemption, climaxing in the death and resurrection of Jesus, is God's strategy to bring about a just and lasting peace between rebel man and Himself, and then between man and man. Therefore, God's children are that way, too. They have the character of their Father. What he loves, they love. What he pursues, they pursue. You can know his children by whether they are willing to make sacrifices for peace the way God did.

JOHN PIPER

Being a peace catalyst is a long, arduous and often lonesome journey. We need fellow pilgrims to join us and help us along the way. We need to learn conflict resolution skills. But to embody peace and fruitfully pursue peace for the long haul, we need more than just peacemaking practices. We need "to unite a deep vision with . . . concrete skills, virtues and habits."[1] One of the best ways to develop a deep vision is to grasp the big picture of God's peace purposes.

This is what happened to me. I pride myself on knowing the Bible, but as I studied the topic of peace from Genesis to Revelation, I realized that the idea of peace and peacemaking is much bigger than I thought. I wondered how I had missed it. The stories and principles I now see in Scripture provide the substance for what I write about in this chapter. What I discovered transformed my life. I hope it does the same for you.

The simple diagram in figure 2.1 illustrates the biblical framework for peacemaking described in this book. It captures the theological heart of peacemaking and many of the practices that emerge from it. But even a great diagram cannot depict the comprehensive complexity of waging peace in practice.

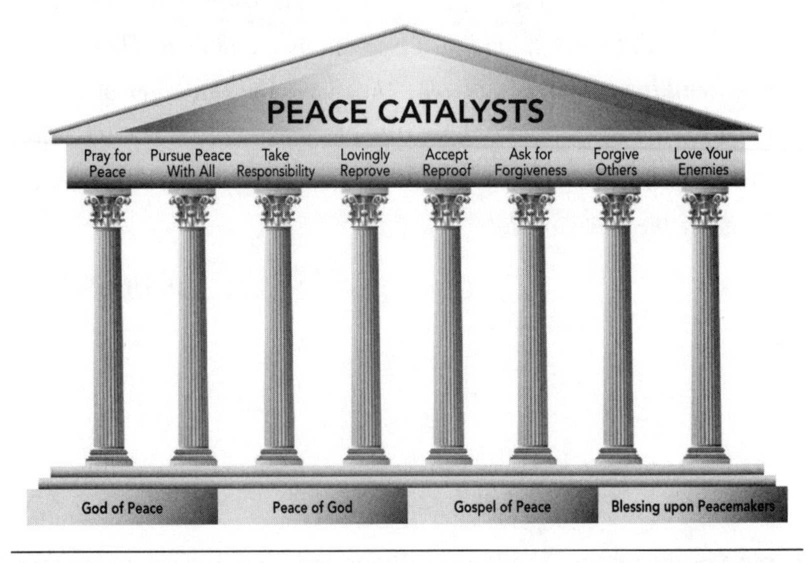

Figure 2.1

I will outline the breadth and depth of God's work of peace in the world using the four foundation stones and eight pillars in this illustration. The four foundation stones teach that peacemakers are blessed to represent the God of Peace, pursue the peace of God and share the gospel of peace. The eight pillars of peacemaking exhort us to pray for peace and take practical steps to pursue peace with everyone. This section may be a little heavy theologically, but it is worth it if you really want to be a peace catalyst.

I only wish I had known these things about peacemaking forty years ago, when I started following Jesus. In some sense I feel ripped off because I was not taught most of these fundamental truths in the churches I attended. May you examine the Scripture to see for yourself, and may you experience your conversion to peace (if you haven't already).

THE GOD OF PEACE

At the deepest level, our desire for and the practices of peacemaking are built on God's character and heart for peace. In this chapter we will examine the first two foundation stones of peacemaking: the God of Peace and the peace of God.

The Bible portrays God as the God of Peace (or a comparable title) ten times. God is the source and giver of peace. This is one of the most frequent and important titles for God in the Bible.[2]

Judges 6:11-24 recounts the call and commission of Gideon, as a story about the God of Peace. Yahweh's recruiting angel promises to be with Gideon and to empower him to deliver Israel from the oppression of the Midianites. But Gideon asks for a sign that God is truly speaking. When the angel of the Lord consumes his offering by fire, Gideon shrinks back in fear, realizing he had come face to face with the angel of the Lord. God then comforts Gideon by speaking peace to him: "The LORD said to him, 'Peace! Do not be afraid. You are not going to die'" (v. 23). This promise of peace (*shalom*) assured Gideon that God was indeed speaking and that God would give him success and well-being.[3] "So Gideon built an altar to the LORD there and called it The LORD Is Peace" (Judges 6:24).

In one of the most well-known prophecies in the Bible, Isaiah describes the person of the coming Messiah and the nature of his kingdom. He is the Prince of Peace, and his promised kingdom will be a kingdom of peace, justice and righteousness:

> For to us a child is born, to us a son is given, and the government will be on his shoulders. And he will be called Wonderful Counselor, Mighty God, Everlasting Father, Prince of Peace. Of the increase of his government and peace there will be no end. He will reign on David's throne and over his kingdom, establishing and upholding it with justice and righteousness from that time on and forever. The zeal of the LORD Almighty will accomplish this. (Isaiah 9:6-7)

The title God of Peace finds frequent expression in prayer:

- "The God of peace be with you all. Amen" (Romans 15:33).
- "May God himself, the God of peace, sanctify you through and through" (1 Thessalonians 5:23).
- "Now may the Lord of peace himself give you peace at all times and in every way. The Lord be with all of you" (2 Thessalonians 3:16).

Peace at all times and at every way? I pray this a lot.

In a few cases Paul uses the title when he writes about division and disorder in the church. He highlights this aspect of God's character in order to strengthen his exhortation:

- "The God of peace will soon crush Satan under your feet" (Romans 16:20).
- "For God is not a God of disorder but of peace" (1 Corinthians 14:33).
- "Finally, brothers and sisters, rejoice! Strive for full restoration, encourage one another, be of one mind, live in peace. And the God of love and peace will be with you" (2 Corinthians 13:11).

The author of Hebrews does the same thing. He alludes to strained relationships between the leaders and the house church and then prays: "May the God of peace, who through the blood of the eternal covenant brought back from the dead our Lord Jesus, that great Shepherd of the sheep, equip you with everything good for doing his will, and may he work in us what is pleasing to him, through Jesus Christ, to whom be glory for ever and ever. Amen" (Hebrews 13:20-21).

Finally, Paul uses the title once to address anxiety and encourage personal peace:

> Do not be anxious about anything, but in every situation, by prayer and petition, with thanksgiving, present your requests to God. And the peace of God, which transcends all understanding, will guard your hearts and your minds. . . . Whatever you have learned or received or heard from me, or seen in me—put it into practice. And the God of peace will be with you. (Philippians 4:6-7, 9 NIV)

We often put titles on business cards to describe who we are and to add credibility. For example, one of my titles is "Consultant for Christian-Muslim Relations." If God were handing out business cards, it would say, "Yahweh: God of Peace." God's calling card is peace.

The God of Peace dwells in us and finds expression through us. *We* represent the God of Peace in a world of hostility and conflict. This truth helps us persevere when we face difficult disputes and divisions. When we feel like giving up, we need to remind ourselves that our God is the God of Peace. In a world battered by violence and war, we need to remind ourselves of this important title. Miroslav Volf rightly notes, "Violence is not human destiny, because the God of peace is the beginning and the end of human history."[4]

THE PEACE OF GOD

The second foundation stone of peacemaking is the peace, or shalom, of God. *Shalom* is the Hebrew term for peace. A quick review of the 250 or so occurrences of *shalom* in the Hebrew Scriptures shows that God's peace is multidimensional and comprehensive. This one word has been variously translated as *peace*, *prosperity*, *success*, *well-being*, *safety*, *welfare*, *health*, *deliverance*, *salvation* and *completeness*.

The meaning of shalom encompasses social justice. How can I say this? Because it is impossible to live in a state of peace, safety and well-being if one experiences injustice and oppression.[5] Isaiah's prophecy of the future messianic kingdom demonstrates the profound connection between shalom and social justice: "Of the increase of his government and peace [shalom] there will be no end. He will reign on David's throne and over his kingdom, establishing and upholding it with justice and righteousness" (Isaiah 9:7).

Isaiah uses what scholars call synonymous parallelism to define this coming kingdom. In other words, the meaning in the first line is expressed in different but equivalent terms in the second. Thus the first line, "his government and peace," means roughly the same thing as the second, "his kingdom, establishing and upholding it with justice and righteousness." This same kind of parallelism between shalom and justice/righteousness is found repeatedly in the Old Testament (see Isaiah 32:17-18; 59:8; 60:17; Psalm 72:3,7; 85:10; Zechariah 8:16-19).

Nicholas Wolterstorff describes well this overlap in meaning: "In shalom, each person enjoys justice, enjoys his or her rights. There is no shalom without justice. But shalom goes beyond justice. Shalom is the human being dwelling at peace in all his or her relationships."[6] Thus shalom is turbocharged peace, full-spectrum peace, peace amplified. It involves the transformation of the personal, social and structural dimensions of life. Shalom includes human flourishing in all dimensions of life.[7]

Cornelius Plantinga's definition captures both the beauty and the breadth of shalom:

> The webbing together of God, humans, and all creation in justice, fulfillment, and delight is what the Hebrew prophets call shalom. We call it peace, but it means far more than mere peace of mind or a cease-fire between enemies. In the Bible, shalom means universal flourishing, wholeness, and delight. . . . Shalom, in other words, is the way things ought to be.[8]

Jeremiah's exhortation to the Jews in Babylon provides a riveting description of how to make shalom: "Seek the shalom of the city where I have sent you into exile, and pray to the LORD on its behalf; for in its shalom you will have shalom" (Jeremiah 29:7, my translation).

Imagine the impact of Jeremiah's exhortation on the Jewish exiles. The Babylonians were the enemies—their captors and oppressors. Psalm 137:8-9 gives us a snapshot of the seething hatred of the Jews toward the Babylonians: "O Babylon, you will be destroyed. Happy is the one who pays you back for what you have done to us. Happy is the one who takes your babies and smashes them against the rocks!" (NLT).

Yet God commands the Jews to seek the peace of Babylon. Basically he tells them to love their enemies, the very ones who had so cruelly oppressed them. This was astounding. No one in recorded history ever said anything like it—until Jesus came on the scene six centuries later and said, "You have heard that it was said, 'Love your neighbor and hate your enemy.' But I tell you, love your enemies and pray for those who persecute you, that you may be children of your Father in heaven" (Matthew 5:43-45).

In Scripture, Babylon epitomizes evil. But even in the context of the "evil empire," God commanded the Jewish exiles to pursue and pray for his comprehensive shalom. He challenged these forlorn refugees to become fruitful residents. Along with these commands is a promise: as they worked for the shalom of the city, they too would experience shalom.

Jeremiah's great command portrays a vision for human flourishing—for all. God was calling the Jewish exiles to seek the common good of the cities where they lived. In New Testament terms, God was calling them to be salt and light, to glorify him through their loving deeds of service to those outside of the faith (Matthew 5:13-16).

Jeremiah 29:7 describes how personal faith intersects with public life, illustrated elsewhere in the Old Testament most profoundly in the lives of Joseph, Daniel and Esther.[9] This verse shows how believers engage with nonbelievers for the sake of the common good. It provides us with a paradigm for ministry. "Seek the shalom of the city" shows us how to minister in the urban world of the twenty-first century, where over half of the world lives.[10]

Following Jesus into the cities of the world will lead us to culture shapers, diverse ethnic groups and the poorest of the poor. Because of this, shalom makers partner with local governments, businesses and interested parties to enhance the quality of life for everyone. They seek racial reconciliation and harmony between different religious communities. And they serve the poor and work to alleviate poverty.

Pursuing the shalom of the city also includes caring for creation. Overcrowded cities especially suffer from environmental pollution.[11] Toxic air, dirty water and contaminated soil negatively impact the quality of life. The degradation of creation stifles human flourishing for everyone. And the poor suffer the most. Millions of children in the poorest cities of the world will not live to see their fifth birthday because of diseases such as diarrhea, malaria and respiratory illnesses caused by environmental degradation.

The world is out of harmony with God's good creation. So shalom makers help people live in harmony with creation by stopping and preventing activities that pollute our planet. Pursuing shalom means we work for ecological harmony and wholeness. Because we worship and honor the Creator, we seek to cultivate and protect creation. In doing so we help bring shalom to earth.

I have gone into great detail about shalom to help us understand its meaning. But textual analysis alone doesn't always help us sense its beauty. I was leading a family Bible study at Christmas almost two decades ago, and we were talking about Jesus as the Prince of Shalom. I wanted to help my daughters feel the significance of shalom, so I asked, "What does it mean practically when Jesus brings shalom?" Ever the preacher, I had to answer: "Shalom is what you feel when you are watching a movie and you get a tear in your eye. It's that sense of goodness you experience when you watch a heartwarming scene."

Think about it. Most scenes that touch us emotionally depict something beautiful. Courageous soldiers sacrifice their lives to save others.

A husband brings flowers to his estranged wife and asks for forgiveness. Someone recovers from a serious illness. People come together in an emergency to help one another. The good guys triumph over the bad guys. Why do scenes like these touch us so deeply? Because, for that brief moment, we sense something deep within our souls: *this is the way things ought to be*. Our hearts dance. We get teary-eyed. We have tasted of shalom and it is good![12]

Just how important are God's peace purposes for this world? Important enough that God repeatedly sent prophets to predict the future messianic reign of peace. God wants us to know it, to set our hope on it and to get excited about it. These peace predictions function something like a chorus in a good song. We circle back to the heart of the song repeatedly so we don't miss the point. God wants this Old Testament peace refrain to stick in our minds.

Both Micah and Zechariah predicted a future ruler whose reign would be characterized by shalom. This coming king would usher in a kingdom of peace.[13] Ezekiel spoke of a coming king and a future covenant of peace—referring to the new covenant.[14]

> My servant David will be king over them, and they will all have one shepherd. . . . I will make a covenant of peace with them; it will be an everlasting covenant. I will establish them and increase their numbers, and I will put my sanctuary among them forever. My dwelling place will be with them; I will be their God, and they will be my people. (Ezekiel 37:24, 26-27 NIV; see also 34:23-27)

Both Isaiah and Micah portrayed the coming kingdom of peace as a restoration of God's original creation purposes. Even when the word *shalom* is not used, they pictured a future that was perfectly nonviolent, innocent and harmonious. They foresaw a world where the enmity and alienation separating the nations since Babel was undone (Genesis 11). They saw the nations under God's reign: hostility ended, reconciliation achieved and prosperity experienced; harmony between all creation restored. God's endgame is comprehensive peace.

> In the last days the mountain of the LORD's temple will be established as the highest of the mountains. . . . He will judge between the nations and will settle disputes for many peoples. They will beat their swords into plowshares and their spears into pruning hooks. Nation will not take up sword against nation, nor will they train for war anymore. (Isaiah 2:2, 4; see also Micah 4:1-3)

> The wolf will live with the lamb, the leopard will lie down with the goat, the calf and the lion and the yearling together; and a little child will lead them. The cow will feed with the bear, their young will lie down together, and the lion will eat straw like the ox. Infants will play near the hole of the cobra; young children will put their hands into the viper's nest. They will neither harm nor destroy on all my holy mountain, for the earth will be filled with the knowledge of the LORD as the waters cover the sea. (Isaiah 11:6-9)

> "See, I will create new heavens and a new earth. . . . The wolf and the lamb will feed together, and the lion will eat straw like the ox, but dust will be the serpent's food. They will neither harm nor destroy on all my holy mountain," says the LORD. (Isaiah 65:17, 25)

What does all this future stuff about peace have to do with our lives right now? Is there any practical relevance? Does it only describe the hope we have in the age to come? No! This future kingdom of peace has relevance now.

One of the greatest promises of God's peace (shalom) in the Hebrew Scriptures is found in Isaiah 52:7: "How lovely on the mountains / Are the feet of him who brings good news, / Who announces peace / And brings good news of happiness, / Who announces salvation, / And says to Zion, 'Your God reigns!'" (NASB).

Isaiah spoke of the good news of a coming kingdom. This is explicit in the final phrase "Your God reigns" (which is another way of talking about the kingdom). And how did Isaiah describe God's reign? In three ways: as peace (shalom), as happiness (or goodness) and as salvation. As the prominent Old Testament scholar Chris Wright says, "When God reigns, there will be peace, life will be good and we will be saved."[15]

This promise in Isaiah was quoted or clearly alluded to five times in the New Testament (Acts 10:36; Romans 10:15; 2 Corinthians 5:20; Ephesians 2:17; 6:15), providing vital background information for understanding Jesus' mission. It sheds important light on the meaning of Jesus' central message—the kingdom of God.

In the life, death and resurrection of Jesus, the kingdom of God has been launched on earth. As he taught us to pray, "Your kingdom come, your will be done, on earth as it is in heaven" (Matthew 6:10). There is no disease in heaven, so we work toward the elimination of disease here on earth through hospitals and medicine. There is no slavery in heaven, so we work to abolish it on earth. There is no war or injustice in heaven, so we work toward shalom in the here and now.

This kingdom of peace, happiness and salvation comes in two stages. There was present, partial fulfillment at the first coming of Christ. But we also look forward to a complete, perfect fulfillment at the second coming of Christ. The kingdom of God is both present *and* future, "already" *and* "not yet."

The already of the kingdom refers to the rule and reign of God in the lives of Jesus' followers. It means that the kingdom of God comes on earth now through us. When we share the good news of King Jesus, when we heal the sick or cast out demons and when we do works of righteousness, peacemaking, justice and mercy *in Jesus' name,* the kingdom comes. The gospel of the kingdom is not just about getting people into heaven. It's also about bringing heaven to earth.[16]

The prominent New Testament scholar N. T. Wright put it like this: "The Beatitudes are the agenda for kingdom people. . . . They are about the way in which Jesus wants to rule the world. He wants to do it *through* this sort of people. . . . When God wants to change the world, he doesn't send in the tanks. He sends in the meek, the mourners, those who are hungry and thirsty for God's justice, the peacemakers, and so on."[17]

All the prophecies about a future kingdom of peace should fill us with hope. But they also describe what God wants to do in or through us in the present. "For the kingdom of God is not a matter of eating and drinking, but of righteousness, peace and joy in the Holy Spirit" (Romans 14:17).

In 2011, my wife, Fran, and I went to the Philippines to minister at a Vineyard conference. One evening our Filipino hosts set up over twenty dinner tables end to end with no chairs around them. There were no forks, spoons or knives. An assortment of delicious dishes served as the centerpiece for what they call the Boodle feast. We stood across from each other, ate with our hands and talked. This tradition was popularized by the Philippine Military Academy in Baguio City and is primarily done as a form of fellowship and camaraderie between officers and military personnel, no matter what rank. A similar practice is common when Filipinos go camping. They take their packed lunch and put it on a table or the ground over some banana leaves and share it with everyone around.[18]

The kingdom of God may not be a matter of eating or drinking, but in the Philippines, eating and drinking serves as a wonderful way to break down barriers and build bridges. Hospitality like this is one way we can pursue peace. I think that's why much of Jesus' ministry took place over food.

The God of Peace and the peace of God are not merely footnotes in the Bible's story. They parade around on center stage. And how do we experience this God of Peace and the peace of God? Through the gospel of peace—the third foundation stone of peacemaking.

THE GOSPEL OF PEACE

The Prince of Peace entered the world to usher in God's shalom to a broken, alienated world. The gospel is explicitly referred to as the "gospel of peace" five times in the New Testament, indicating the close relationship between the gospel and peacemaking (Acts 10:36; Ephesians 2:13-17; 6:15; Colossians 1:20; Romans 5:1).

As we have seen in the first two foundation stones, peace is a far more comprehensive concept than we usually realize. The gospel of peace is no different. When we think of the gospel, we primarily think of experiencing peace with God, as illustrated in Romans 5:1: "Therefore, since we have been justified through faith, we have peace with God through our Lord Jesus Christ."

Peace with God is a vital part of the gospel. And it is essential to building a life of peacemaking. But we lose much of the richness of the gospel if we make it only about peace with God.

The gospel of peace was first preached to a man of war. God supernaturally led the apostle Peter to the home of the Roman centurion Cornelius (Acts 10). Cornelius was just the kind of person Peter didn't want to share with. Cornelius was a Gentile; he lived in the wrong place—Caesarea (the Roman capital of the province of Judea)—and he was the enemy, an occupying soldier. These are some of the reasons it took three God-inspired visions before Peter was willing to meet with him.

What was Peter's message? "You know the message God sent to the people of Israel, announcing the good news of peace through Jesus Christ, who is Lord of all" (Acts 10:36). In this context, the peace of the gospel includes reconciliation both with God and with neighbor. It is multidimensional. As preachers like to point out, the cross of Christ has both vertical and horizontal beams, indicating the twofold nature of this reconciliation. The gospel was and is a force of transformation in the lives of both the bearer and the receiver of the good news.

Remember Isaiah's prophecy of the wolf and the lamb living in harmony (Isaiah 11:6)? We see this in the gospel of peace: Cornelius, the "wolf" of Roman occupation, and Peter, a follower of the lamb of God, are united in Christ. This is why we preach and live the gospel of peace: we are continuing Jesus' work of ushering in the kingdom of God, which is a kingdom of peace.

Cornelius's story demonstrates what Paul later taught about the gospel of peace in Ephesians.

> But now in Christ Jesus you who once were far away have been brought near through the blood of Christ. For he himself is our peace, who has made the two one. . . . His purpose was to create in himself one new man out of the two, thus making peace, and in one body to reconcile both of them to God through the cross. . . . He came and preached peace to you who were far away and peace to those who were near. (Ephesians 2:13-17)

Through Christ's death, Jews and Gentiles have experienced a double reconciliation. They have been reconciled to God and to one another. According to Paul, Jesus is our peace. Jesus makes peace. Jesus proclaims peace.

One can hardly overemphasize how radical this message of peace must have sounded to Paul's original audience. The relationship between Gentile and Jew could be described as a prototype of all division or racial alienation in the first century—comparable to the relationship between whites and blacks in the United States before the civil rights movement or in South Africa under apartheid. The animosity felt between most Americans and Muslims since 9/11 serves as a more up-to-date example.

Through the gospel, the church becomes an alternative society, a community where humanity's divisions have been overcome—a foretaste of heaven's harmony. Anything less would be a denial of the gospel and nature of the church. We've got some work to do here!

Paul extends our understanding of the breadth of God's peace purposes even further in Colossians: "For God was pleased to have all his fullness dwell in him [Jesus], and through him to reconcile to himself all things, whether things on earth or things in heaven, by making peace through his blood, shed on the cross" (Colossians

1:19-20). The scope of Christ's reconciliation is breathtaking. We've seen how the gospel of peace brings reconciliation with God and reconciliation with both neighbor and enemy (sometimes they're the same person). But in this verse we see that reconciliation extends to both heavenly and earthly realities—a promise of universal and cosmic peace. The reconciling purpose at the cross was to restore humanity to fellowship with God and to restore the harmony of the original creation. The disharmonies of nature and the injustices in the world have begun to be put right through the peacemaking work of Jesus on the cross.[19]

There's another passage every peacemaker needs to understand: Galatians 3:26-28, a text that displays the peacemaking nature of the gospel without mentioning the word *peace* (or *reconciliation*). "So in Christ Jesus you are all children of God through faith, for all of you who were baptized into Christ have clothed yourselves with Christ. There is neither Jew nor Gentile, neither slave nor free, neither male nor female, for you are all one in Christ Jesus."

The background to this passage illumines its profound social implications. Paul showed that the gospel counters the prevailing and demeaning attitude of society summarized in a prayer he used to offer up every day as a Jew: "Blessed are you O Lord God, for you have not made me a Greek, you have not made me a woman, and you have not made me a slave." Persians and Greeks offered up similar prayers.[20]

These prayers deny the clear biblical teaching about human dignity and the sacredness of human life.[21] But they give us insight into the prejudices of Jews and Greeks toward particular segments of society at that time. So Paul showed that Christ's reconciling purposes break down barriers between the three great divisions in the ancient (and modern) world: race (Jew and Gentile), class (slave and free) and gender (male and female).

The phrase "all of you who were baptized into Christ" (Galatians 3:27) implies that verse 28 was part of a baptismal formula, underscoring its significance. Imagine how profound our baptism services would be if we reflected on the socially explosive implications of the gospel. Alexander Venter, a Vineyard pastor in South Africa, tells how his church made this part of their practice. During their baptismal services they confess: "I am no longer black nor white, rich nor poor, male nor female. I am now one in Jesus Christ and His people."[22]

Jesus breaks down divisions between Jew and Gentile, slave and free, and male and female. He brings unity and equality among us all.

MULTIDIMENSIONAL RECONCILIATION IN AFRICA

I was in a country in Africa where white Arabs routinely oppressed black Africans. I was asked to speak to a small group of leaders from both ethnic groups who were new followers of Jesus. When I entered the room, I was thrilled with the ethnic diversity of Christ's followers. There were a few Americans, a brother from Switzerland and a brother from Hong Kong, along with Arabs and members of one African tribe. My words were translated from English into two other languages, so the message didn't move quickly.

As the gray-bearded "sheikh" from America, I was the honored guest. These leaders went out of their way to serve me and show me respect. I read from John 13 and discussed the story of Jesus washing the feet of his disciples. Then I asked them to imagine what it would be like if Jesus walked into the room and washed their feet. After they had served me so vigorously, the impact of Jesus' actions was palpable.

I quoted John 13:14-17: "Now that I, your Lord and Teacher, have washed your feet, you also should wash one another's feet. I have set you an example that you should do as I have done for you. . . . You will be blessed if you do." They did not miss the radical nature of Jesus' example. I asked, "What do you think Jesus expects of you in light of this passage?"

There was an awkward moment of silence because of the history of conflict between the two groups. Then one of the Arabs spoke up. "I think we need to greet each other when we meet on the street," he said. Another answered, "We need to show unbelievers that we are different."

The conversation turned to their need to build relationships and love one another even though there were years of hostility and oppression. The gospel was breaking down the barriers of the dividing wall of hostility. I believe the angels of heaven rejoiced and marveled at God's peacemaking plan, while the demons of hell looked on in shock. Here was a foretaste of heaven. Here was an example of the multicultural people of God whom Jesus is bringing together (see Ephesians 3 for the best description of this).

GOD'S CHILDREN OF PEACE

The fourth and last foundation stone of peacemaking is found in Jesus' famous words "Blessed are the peacemakers, for they will be called children of God" (Matthew 5:9).[23] Jesus pronounced this blessing on peacemakers, which means that God's favor and approval rests on them.

The theme of peacemaking—if not the term—pervades the Sermon on the Mount.[24] The following subjects in Jesus' famous discourse relate directly to the task of peacemaking:

- anger and reconciliation (Matthew 5:21-26)
- not reacting violently against the one who is evil (5:38-42)[25]
- loving one's enemies (5:43-48)
- forgiving (6:12, 14, 15)
- not judging others (7:1-5)

Jesus' use of the terms *opponent* (Matthew 5:25 NASB), *Gentiles* (5:47; 6:7; 6:32 NASB), *enemies* (5:43-44), *unrighteous* (5:45) and *persecute* (5:10, 11, 12, 44) in the Sermon on the Mount indicates that peacemaking is not restricted to believers only. It takes place in an unbelieving world, beyond the boundaries of the church. Thus it relates to broader social and global challenges such as racism, terrorism, poverty and war.

Being a peacemaker is complicated. Peacemakers place a priority on common ground. They learn to develop a bias toward compromise on unimportant issues. They defuse hostility and seek concord by believing the best about people and by putting the best interpretation on others' motives and actions.[26]

When evangelicals talk about being children of God, they rightly quote John 1:12: "Yet to all who did receive him, to those who believed in his name, he gave the right to become children of God." I rarely hear evangelicals describe God's children as peacemakers. But Jesus did. They were called children of God because they act like their Father: the God of Peace (Philippians 4:9; 1 Thessalonians 5:23), who sent the Prince of Peace (Isaiah 9:6) to bring about a world of peace (Luke 2:14). Peacemakers imitate God. God's children are children of peace.

The God of Peace, the peace of God, the gospel of peace and the blessing on peacemakers are the four foundation stones of peacemaking. If we change the order a bit, we could summarize how we live this out: As God's blessed children, we work for peace. We represent the God of Peace. We pursue the peace of God. We share the gospel of peace.

THE QUESTION OF THE SWORD

When I speak about the blessing of being a peacemaker, people often counter with this question: "Yes, but Jesus also said he did not come to bring peace but a sword [see Matthew 10:34]. So how do you reconcile these two verses?"

It is helpful to look at the broader context of both texts. Matthew 5:9 is part of the section in Matthew describing the *ethics* of the kingdom, whereas Matthew 10:34 is found in the section referring to the *mission* of the kingdom. The ethics of the kingdom and the mission of the kingdom are not in tension. The mission of the kingdom is carried out in harmony with the ethics of the kingdom. In fact, that is exactly what Jesus taught.

Matthew 10 described Jesus' commission of his disciples to extend the kingdom. Before any mention of a sword, he told them to go in peace: "If the house is worthy, give it your blessing of peace. But if it is not worthy, take back your blessing of peace" (Matthew 10:13 NASB). When Jesus sent out the seventy disciples, he described this process in a slightly different way: "Whatever house you enter, first say, 'Peace be to this house.' If a man of peace is there, your peace will rest on him; but if not, it will return to you" (Luke 10:5-6 NASB).[27]

This passage implies that in some sense those on mission are bearers of peace (see John 14:27), whose fruitfulness depends on the discernment of peace when sharing their faith. While the practical implications of how to do this needs to be verified through further experience and reflection, no one who takes Scripture seriously can doubt that peace is related to bearing witness.

The second mention of peace in Matthew 10 relates to persecution and suffering brought about because of fruitful witness:

> Do not suppose that I have come to bring peace to the earth. I did not come to bring peace, but a sword. For I have come to turn 'a man against his father, a daughter against her mother, a daughter-in-law against her mother-in-law—a man's enemies will be the members of his own household.' Anyone who loves their father or mother more than me is not worthy of me; anyone who loves their son or daughter more than me is not worthy of me. Whoever does not take up their cross and follow me is not worthy of me. (Matthew 10:34-38 NIV)

Jesus' followers are peacemaking witnesses who speak the blessing of peace on families where they stay. Nevertheless, response to the message of the kingdom will be mixed; some will accept the message, others will reject it. Because of this, conflict will ensue and families will be divided.[28] But please note: Jesus used the metaphor of the sword to describe the divisive fallout that sometimes accompanies the extension of the kingdom. This is confirmed by the parallel passage in Luke: "Do you think I came to bring peace on earth? No, I tell you, but division" (Luke 12:51). Jesus did not use the metaphor of the sword to depict any form of violence or belligerence on the part of his followers.[29]

For many evangelicals, Matthew 10:34-38 ("I did not come to bring peace") rather than Matthew 5:9 ("Blessed are the peacemakers") seems to provide the dominant perspective regarding peace and witness in the New Testament. In other words, there is the assumption that conflict will prevail. With this mindset, could it be that conflict sometimes ensues because of the non-irenic manner in which we communicate the message? Could this be something of a self-fulfilling prophecy?

How do we reconcile Matthew 10:34-38 with Matthew 5:9? At the very least, we need to affirm both truths, since the Bible does. In their book *Hard Sayings of the Bible*, W. C. Kaiser, Peter H. Davids, F. F. Bruce and Manfred T. Brauch give wise guidance: "When Jesus said that he had come to bring 'not peace but a sword' he meant that this would be the *effect* of his coming, not that it was the *purpose* of his coming."[30] As children of God, our purpose is to represent the Prince of Peace, regardless of the effect it has.

ST. FRANCIS OF ASSISI: LIVING AND SHARING THE GOSPEL OF PEACE

One of the best examples of a peacemaking witness is St. Francis of Assisi. Myths, stories and caricatures abound regarding St. Francis of Assisi. Some see him as the patron saint of ecology, others as the model peacemaker. But one thing is clear about his life: he resisted the status quo when it came to Christian-Muslim relations. He opposed the violence of the Crusades and wanted to end the senseless bloodshed. St. Francis was a man of peace who shared the gospel of peace.

His attitude toward Muslims (called Saracens at that time) was exceptional. As one biographer put it, "There was a small, insignificant man from Assisi who dared to oppose the church policy."[31] Instead of fighting, he courageously went with his fellow monk Illuminato to share his faith with the sultan of Egypt, Malik Al-Kamil.[32] The details of his personal outreach remain sketchy, but there is consensus on most of the main points of this peacemaking and evangelistic encounter.

On the way to visit the sultan, Francis and Illuminato purportedly saw two sheep browsing tranquilly, which they took to be a sign of divine providence. Francis reminded Illuminato of Christ's words to his disciples: "I am sending you out like sheep among wolves" (Matthew 10:16). The "wolves" fell upon them soon afterward as they were captured and beaten by the sultan's army. Eventually their captors took them to the sultan.

Sultan Malik Al-Kamil asked his prisoners why they had come, whether they were messengers or Christians who wanted to become Muslims. Francis replied, "Muslims we shall never become, but we are messengers from God and are here to save your soul." Taken back by their audacity but charmed by their winsomeness, the sultan gathered the Muslim clerics to hear them out. Francis repeatedly pleaded for their conversion and for the end to the fighting. After listening, some of the Muslim clerics urged the sultan to have Francis and Illuminato beheaded.

The sultan resisted the counsel of the clerics, saying, "Those men commanded me, in the name of God and of the law, to have your heads cut off, because the law commands it. But I shall ignore this order because it would be a poor recompense for your having come here at the risk of your lives to save my soul." St. Francis and Illuminato were treated as honored guests and finally returned in safety because the sultan believed they would plead the cause of peace.

> Francis went expecting martyrdom and returned safely. Sultan Al-Kamil was friendly and listened to him. Franciscans were free to go into the Sultan's lands after this and were welcomed and

heard provided they did not preach against Muhammad and the Qur'an. It was the same Sultan Al-Kamil who negotiated a peaceful settlement with Frederick II of Sicily when the next crusade threatened. . . . We might infer that Francis' short time with the Sultan achieved a measure of freedom for the Gospel in Muslim lands, and that it probably also had some effect in terms of peacemaking.[33]

3

WHAT PEACE CATALYSTS DO

PART ONE: BECOMING PEACEMAKERS

Jesus does not limit the peacemaking to only one kind, and neither will his disciples. In the light of the gospel, Jesus himself is the supreme peacemaker, making peace between God and man, and man and man. Our peacemaking will include the promulgation of that gospel. It must also extend to seeking all kinds of reconciliation. Instead of delighting in division, bitterness, strife, or some petty "divide and conquer" mentality, disciples of Jesus delight to make peace wherever possible.

D. A. CARSON

PEACE BREAKERS, PEACE FAKERS AND PEACEMAKERS

Chances are, since you are reading this book, you want to be a peacemaker. You want to learn about the peace Christ models, promises and commands. You want to embody Jesus' teaching on conflict resolution. Yet good intentions and loving aspirations frequently fail in the face of conflict. In reality we are often peace breakers. Some of us are by nature peace fakers. Yet in the depths of our being, we all long to be peacemakers.

LET ME DEFINE WHAT I DO AND DO NOT MEAN BY PEACEMAKING

Peacemaking is not peacekeeping. Peacekeepers are conflict avoiders, sweeping important issues under the carpet so no conflict manifests itself. This often happens in families and churches. This also happens between alienated ethnic groups and countries.

Peacekeepers separate two parties in order to prevent conflict and thereby keep the peace. Temporary separation for the sake of de-escalation *is* a valid step in the process of peacemaking during a war and in a radically broken marriage or relationship. When tensions or emotions run high, we need outside help to keep us from explosive reactions.

Peacekeeping is peace *faking*. It is a forced peace; it is a false peace. And God does not like false peace. "They have healed the brokenness of My people superficially, Saying, 'Peace, peace,' But there is no peace" (Jeremiah 6:14 NASB; see also Jeremiah 8:11; Ezekiel 13:10).

True peace is not just the absence of conflict but the presence of harmony.[1] And so peacemakers sometimes need to be peace disturbers. They need to shake things up, expose hidden heart issues or confront barriers to harmony.

The Prince of Peace certainly disturbed the peace of the Pharisees more than once. Jesus relentlessly challenged them about their attitudes of superiority and judgment—two mindsets that divide rather than unite people. Moreover, Jesus said they did not have the love of God in their hearts (John 5:42). He knew that the motivating power of God's love was lacking in the Pharisees and would undermine harmony in relationships.

Martin Luther King Jr. had to do a lot of peace disturbing in the peacemaking effort we call the civil rights movement. King boldly and lovingly addressed the hypocrisy, prejudice and injustices perpetrated by the white establishment against African Americans. But he wasn't just trying to overthrow white supremacy. He sought reconciliation between these two groups. Before there could be peace, the status quo had to be disturbed.

Honest and authentic communication is essential for peace. It is also true, however, that sharing like this often exposes our differences and leads to discord. Having harmony in relationships does not mean that we will always agree with each other. Unity does not mean uniformity.[2] There are times we need to "agree to disagree." Would that we would follow the wise and famous maxim attributed to St. Augustine: "In essentials, unity; in non-essentials, liberty; in all things, charity."[3]

Peacemaking is not peace achieving. We are commanded to pursue peace, but this doesn't mean we will be successful in our efforts. As I noted earlier, Romans 12:18 is realistic about conflict and discord. Biblical peacemaking is neither sentimental nor naive. It addresses the harsh realities of brokenness and evil. Our most sincere efforts may fail because reconciliation demands a response from both parties involved in conflict.

Peacemaking is not peace building. These terms have much in common and are often used interchangeably. But the differences are noteworthy. Peace building refers to proactive initiatives that seek to prevent conflict from occurring or from reoccurring. Thus peace building focuses on conflict prevention, whereas peacemaking focuses on conflict resolution.

The term *peace building* is a central component of the modern study of conflict resolution. But the term itself is not found in Scripture. I believe it is best to understand it as an important subcategory of peacemaking since many verses in the Bible focus on peace building—that is, cultivating loving relationships that result in a culture of peace. A biblical understanding of peacemaking demands a proactive and preventive commitment to both present and future peace (which is how peace building is usually understood).

Peacemaking is more than conflict resolution. I sometimes use the terms *peacemaking* and *conflict resolution* interchangeably, because *conflict resolution* is the term used most frequently in secular literature to describe what I mean by peacemaking. However, the biblical term *peacemaking* has a richer, deeper meaning than is usually associated with conflict resolution. And certainly the practice of biblical peacemaking demands more than the practice of conflict resolution.

Conflict can and usually does take place at three levels: cognitive, emotional and behavioral. We argue over different ideas. We get upset about irritating behaviors. And our feelings get hurt in the process. Because of this, conflict resolution needs to address differences in perspective, emotional hurt and behavioral change. To do so would resolve conflict and restore harmony.

Yet the practice of most conflict resolution does not address all three dimensions. It focuses primarily on behavioral change and only secondarily on the cognitive or the emotional.[4] For example, mediation at the workplace or in a divorce case may result in clear agreement around behavioral goals. But that's all it addresses. In fact, the conflict has been only partially resolved and relational harmony has not been reestablished.

By contrast, biblical peacemaking seeks to resolve conflict at all three levels. This is God's ideal. For example, when the Bible speaks of repentance, it refers to all three dimensions: a change of thinking, feeling and acting. When we confess our sin or apologize, we are not only admitting wrong ideas or actions, we are also expressing remorse for hurting the person. Then we seek to prove our repentance through our deeds (Luke 3:8; Acts 26:20).

I was hired to mediate two different cases of conflict related to missionaries (one in Tanzania in 2012 and one in Brazil in 2013). In both cases I was able to help the parties come up with a written agreement about how they would work together in the future. I successfully fulfilled my role as a mediator.

But those agreements focused primarily on behavioral change and didn't address deeper cognitive or emotional issues. That's why I told both groups before they hired me, "I should wear three hats in this process: as a mediator, a peacemaker and an organizational consultant. As a mediator I can deal with behavioral issues, as a peacemaker I can deal with heart issues and as a consultant I can help with cognitive, or strategic, issues." They agreed and let me serve them in all three capacities. Because of this, I was able to address the cognitive and emotional issues that mediation alone would not address.

I define peacemaking in two separate though important ways: *resolving conflict* and *restoring harmony.* This definition addresses all three levels of conflict previously mentioned and highlights the relational priority of peacemaking. Through repentance, forgiveness and restitution, we resolve our conflicts. Through trust-building actions and practical investments of love we restore and build harmony. Thus true peacemaking goes beyond mere conflict resolution by seeking to reestablish a positive relationship. Understood in this way, peacemaking and reconciliation are often synonymous.

However, there are some important differences between peacemaking and reconciliation. Reconciliation involves at least two parties overcoming their alienation and restoring their broken relationship. By contrast, peacemaking can be carried out by only one party. Peacemakers can make the first steps toward reconciliation with others, even if the other party does not respond.

For example, in a marriage, one spouse can pursue peace (with no guarantee of reconciliation) through unilateral loving acts. The same is true in larger social conflicts. For example, Peace Catalyst International challenges followers of Christ to take the first steps to breaking down barriers between Christians and Muslims.

PURSUING PEACE AND SEEKING JUSTICE?

Pope Paul VI said, "If you want peace, work for justice." I agree. Seeking justice is a crucial component of making peace. So, what is the relationship between justice and peace? The meaning of justice and its relationship to peace centers on two concepts: shalom and restorative justice.[5]

As we have seen, shalom refers to human flourishing in all dimensions and thus includes justice. In other words, the struggle for justice needs to be understood within the overarching framework of God's reconciling purposes. The scales of God's justice tip in the direction of loving relationships.

After the fall of apartheid in South Africa, Archbishop Desmond Tutu led his country in the Truth and Reconciliation Commission (TRC). The TRC rejected the two extremes normally implemented after such violence. There would be no blanket amnesty, nor would every perpetrator face military tribunals as war criminals, such as took place after World War II. They opted for a third way: "granting amnesty to individuals in exchange for a full disclosure relating to the crime for which amnesty was being sought."[6]

This third way was based on the concept of restorative justice that was part of traditional African culture. As Tutu wrote, "The central concern is the healing of breaches, the redressing of imbalances, the restoration of broken relationships, a seeking to rehabilitate both the victim and the perpetrator, who should be given the opportunity to be reintegrated into the community he has injured by his offense."[7]

When people in the West think of justice, they usually think in terms of retribution. We focus on punishment of wrongdoing proportionate to the crime—an eye for an eye and a tooth for a tooth. Retributive justice uses an adversarial approach to justice and curbs the excesses of revenge.

By contrast, restorative justice focuses on both the reparation of harm done and the healing of relationships. It is concerned about the needs of both the victims and the offenders. It uses a collaborative approach to justice and seeks reconciliation. The prophet Micah asked, "What does the LORD require of you?" And then answered: "To act justly" (Micah 6:8). So, what does justice require? There are two different answers to this question (see table 3.1).[8]

Table 3.1

Crime is a violation of the law and the state.	Crime is a violation of people and relationships.
Violations create guilt.	Violations create obligations.
Justice requires the state to determine blame (guilt) and impose pain (punishment.)	Justice involves victim, offenders and community members in an effort to put things right.
Central focus: offenders getting what they deserve.	**Central focus:** victims' needs and offenders' responsibility for repairing harm.

So, what does restorative justice look like in practice? Here's Katy Hutchison's story:

> On December 31st, 1997 my husband Bob excused himself briefly from our small dinner party to check on a teen's house party taking place down the street at the home of a vacationing friend. He never returned. Bob was beaten to death as he attempted to break up the party and I was left widowed with two small children. It took an undercover police operation to break the code of silence that shrouded the small town we lived in, and finally, five years later an arrest was made. Police were stunned by my request to meet the young man who was charged in connection with Bob's death. That face-to-face meeting was the first step in forever changing my perception of real justice.
>
> Being the family victim of a violent crime jettisoned me into the criminal justice system; and a series of processes in which I had little or no say. When I initiated a meeting with the perpetrator I was able to ask the questions I needed answered and regain a sense of control.
>
> Bob's death was tragic and senseless. I couldn't imagine who could be capable of committing such a brutal act. But when I sat across the room from the young man charged with the crime I saw a neighbor, a son, a brother; someone's best friend. His actions were abhorrent, but he was human. Understanding the distinction helped me focus on what support to lobby for in his rehabilitation.

> Our traditional justice system is heavy on punishment and mired in process. The restorative justice approach is about accountability and healing; responding directly and specifically to the needs of the individuals and communities involved. Who better than the victim to describe to the perpetrator the impact of the harm.
>
> Eight years have passed since I sat across from that young man. He has done his time and returned to society committed to his employment, sobriety, pro-social relationships and living safely in his community. There is nothing I could do to bring Bob back, but there was much I could do to support a healthy outcome for the families on both sides of this crime.
>
> After my own experience being directly involved in making justice happen I saw the potential for the restorative process in other aspects of my life. The power of bringing people together to resolve conflict rather than isolating them is my expectation at home, at school, at work and in my community.[9]

So how do we evaluate the strength and weaknesses of retributive and restorative justice? Retributive justice is the focus of much Old Testament law (and most Western legal systems). However, restorative justice better reflects the overall emphasis of Scripture on shalom making and reconciliation.[10] Whereas retributive justice seeks to restrain evil through punishment, restorative justice seeks to overcome evil with good.

Nevertheless, restorative justice is still justice. Chris Marshall writes, "Punishment . . . is an inescapable component of biblical jurisprudence. But the distinctive concern of biblical justice is not to punish sinners, but to restore shalom by clarifying and dealing with the damage caused by wrongdoing."[11]

Restorative justice is not some idealistic Christian theory of justice. It is political and practical: It was implemented in the midst of the blood and brokenness of South Africa. In 1989, New Zealand "made restorative justice the hub of its entire juvenile justice system."[12] In the

United States it is being implemented in the Minnesota criminal justice system and several other states, including where I live, Colorado.[13]

LET THE PEACE OF CHRIST RULE IN YOUR HEARTS

We know that the God of Peace dwells in us and that the Prince of Peace calls us to pursue peace. We rejoice that the gospel produces peace in our lives, and we gratefully acknowledge that God's favor rests on peacemakers. But we still fall short. It is easy for us to become more concerned about winning an argument than we are about making peace. We can become more concerned about looking good than we are about doing what is right. We can become influenced more by the media than we are by the Messiah. Far too many followers of Jesus fear Muslims, hate the LGBT (lesbian, gay, bisexual and transgender) community and despise undocumented immigrants. And in doing so, we lose the peace.

I was talking to a well-known evangelical leader recently. He was sharing that God is helping him walk in greater personal peace. But then he got a bit embarrassed and quickly added, "I don't wanna sound too New Age-ish." I laughed and said, "Bro, I am a peacemaker, and personal or inner peace is part of what it means to follow Jesus. It is not New Age-ish."

To spread the peace, we need to be at peace—peace with God and peace with ourselves. But we have a problem. Our hearts are a battleground, and life is full of peace robbers. How do we apply these stunning truths about God's peace to our lives?

There are no easy answers here. It is not enough to have experienced peace with God in the past. The challenge for each of us is this: What is the state of my heart *today*? How can I be at peace with God and with myself? How can I let the peace of Christ rule in my heart, as the Scripture teaches (Colossians 3:15)?

Let me share four disciplines that help me translate the four foundation stones of peacemaking into my life. They help me get my heart aligned with God's peace purposes, and they may help you.

1. If we rest in God's love, we will live in peace. When I think of the condition of my heart and how it impacts my peacemaking, I recognize that I have to get in touch with God's heart continually. God's great peacemaking initiative in sending Jesus to reconcile us back to himself and to others grew out of his love for us. The "heart" of peacemaking is God's heart (John 3:16; Romans 5:8-11). When I experience God's love, I live in peace.

But resting in God's love doesn't come naturally to me, and I know it doesn't for any of us. Recently I was talking about this with a friend. He said that when he was growing up, all of his life was like a scorecard. Just as basketball players track their rebounds, blocked shots, assists and points per game, my friend felt he needed to track his accomplishments. He wanted to win people's approval. Acceptance depended on his performance. This describes my life, too, except that when I find out what a good score is, I am determined to exceed it. And that is *not* good. But God's love is greater than perfectionism or drivenness.

"Keep yourselves in the love of God," says Jude (Jude 1:21 NASB). What a motivating command! If we are going to keep ourselves in the love of God, we need to think about those things that keep us from God's love. Anxiety, busyness, pride, anger, bitterness, unforgiveness and lack of prayer are just a few ways we block God's love. What other things would you add to this list?

We keep ourselves in God's love by spending time in God's presence; by submitting our lives, our schedules and our relationships to our Lord; by taking a quiet walk in the woods; by enjoying the good gifts God has given to us; by making peace with others. One of my favorite prayers is found in 2 Thessalonians: "May the Lord direct your hearts into God's love and Christ's perseverance" (3:5). When I pray this, I acknowledge that God must do something in my heart. I often repeat the prayer a number of times, inviting God to direct my heart and confessing that I need his love and Christ's steadfastness.

I spend time pondering and praying through this verse. Then I silently sit before the Lord. I am not a very good mystic, but I have learned this: resting in God's love is the opposite of performing for God's approval. When I remind myself that God is love and that we love because he first loved us, all is well with my soul (1 John 4:16, 19). I naturally walk in peace.

2. ***If we walk by faith, we live in peace.*** We often feel buffeted by life's challenges, don't we? The daily grind of family disputes, financial struggles, personal failures, physical illness and the pressure to perform takes its toll on us. And we lose the peace.

The antidote? To pray. "Do not be anxious about anything, but in every situation, by prayer and petition, with thanksgiving, present your requests to God" (Philippians 4:6). First, we must say no to our anxieties. (Did you notice that this is a command?) Next we say yes to God by praying about the things that burden us. We turn our cares into prayers. Finally, we thank God for the good things that come our way. We cultivate a heart of gratefulness. As we pray and as we trust, our anxieties melt away. The result is that God does what only he can do: he gives us peace. "And the peace of God, which transcends all understanding, will guard your hearts and your minds in Christ Jesus" (Philippians 4:7).

Whenever I feel assaulted by anxiety, I meditate on this verse. In fact, I probably pray through Philippians 4:6-7 at least once a week. It helps me to ponder one phrase or sentence at a time and respond in prayer. It goes something like this:

> "Do not be anxious about anything." Okay, Lord, this is a command, and I want to please you. Help me obey.
>
> "In every situation, by prayer and petition, with thanksgiving, present your requests to God." Lord, I begin with thanksgiving. Thank you that I can trust you. Thank you that I can cast my cares on you. Thank you for this opportunity to see you work. Lord, I pray that you will ___________ (I make my requests).
>
> "And the peace of God, which transcends all understanding, will guard your hearts and your minds in Christ Jesus." Lord,

you promised to give me your abundant peace. May your peace transform my thinking. May your peace flood my heart. Now!

3. If we walk in wisdom, we live in peace. King Solomon described wisdom like this: "All her paths are peace" (Proverbs 3:17). In other words, the way of wisdom is the way of peace. Jesus' younger brother James described divine wisdom in the same way: "But the wisdom that comes from heaven is first of all pure; then peace-loving, considerate, submissive, full of mercy and good fruit, impartial and sincere. Peacemakers who sow in peace reap a harvest of righteousness" (James 3:17-18).

Note that the word *peace* is the prominent word (repeated three times) in James's description of God's wisdom. God's wisdom is peace-filled. Wise peacemakers "sow in peace," which means they stay calm and speak without bludgeoning people. There is congruity between their motives and manner, their words and actions.

I usually pray over James 3:17-18 a few times each week. I find it helpful in two ways. First, it helps me evaluate my life. If I am making wise decisions, I will experience peace, since the fruit of wisdom is peace. So if I lack peace, I ask the Lord to show me where I am not walking in his wisdom, and I wait quietly before him. Second, this passage prepares my heart when I face an important meeting, conversation or confrontation. "Lord, I want the beauty of your wisdom to flow through me. Fill me with your heavenly wisdom as I talk with Beverly."

4. If we rid our lives of unnecessary clutter and confusion, we live in peace. This insight makes so much sense practically and could easily be affirmed by believers and nonbelievers alike. But it has an important biblical basis. The church meetings at Corinth were kind of like a circus. People would jump up and speak in tongues or prophesy without any sense of order, causing confusion. Because of this Paul exhorted them to do things decently and in order. The main point of his argument is this: "For God is not a God of disorder but of peace" (1 Corinthians 14:33).

I think this applies to our daily lives as well. When our lives get chaotic or out of control, anxiety gets the upper hand. When my to-do list gets too long and my inbox runneth over, I lose a sense of priorities. I get overwhelmed and I lose the peace. I need to cut things from my schedule. I need to get order in my life, because God is a God of order. My wife, Fran, often says that just having a plan helps her find peace. I agree.

PRAY FOR PEACE

In the following chapters we will turn our attention to developing interpersonal peace practices. I have identified eight specific practices that show us how to proactively pursue peace with everyone. Figure 3.1 is an illustration of these eight pillars of peacemaking.

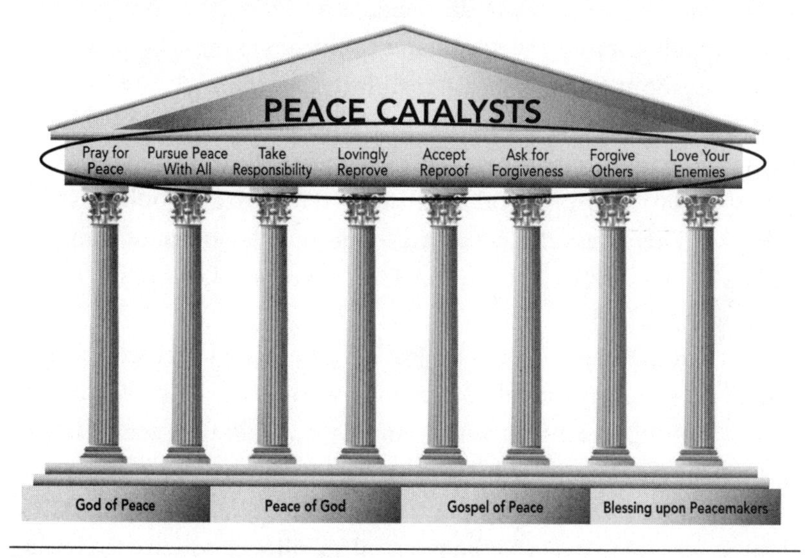

Figure 3.1

The first pillar is pray for peace. Praying for peace is both commanded and modeled throughout the Scriptures. It marks the hidden, behind-the-scenes work of peacemaking. The famous Aaronic benediction is a great example of God's command to bless others with peace: "The

LORD bless you, and keep you; The LORD make His face shine on you, And be gracious to you; The LORD lift up His countenance on you, And give you peace [shalom]" (Numbers 6:24-26 NASB).[14]

Paul the apostle prayed for peace in every one of his letters. He also prayed for peace in every aspect of our lives: "Now may the Lord of peace himself give you peace at all times and in every way" (2 Thessalonians 3:16). I pray this prayer continually for myself and others. If you think this prayer is a little far-fetched, let me remind you what James said: "You do not have because you do not ask" (James 4:2 NKJV). I know that I experience more peace as I pray this prayer. In fact, we might experience more outbreaks of peace if more people prayed like this.

This blessing of peace in all the days and details of our personal lives extends even to the social and political spheres. Look at what Paul says about believers' responsibilities to their society: "I urge, then, first of all, that petitions, prayers, intercession and thanksgiving be made for everyone—for kings and all those in authority, that we may live peaceful and quiet lives in all godliness and holiness. This is good, and pleases God our Savior, who wants all people to be saved and to come to a knowledge of the truth" (1 Timothy 2:1-4).

Ever since I began to follow Jesus at the age of eighteen, I have taken very seriously the call to pray for governments. At early morning prayer meetings, gathered with friends, we would pray for countries around the world, listing by name their kings, presidents and prime ministers. We believed that prayer clout would lead to the political clout necessary to usher in the peaceful stability conducive to sharing the good news of Jesus.

Finally, praying for peace includes resisting the devil. The devil is not only the great deceiver, he is also the great divider, instigating and exacerbating conflict (James 3:15-16; 1 John 3:10-12). He specializes in pouring gasoline on the fires of conflict, deepening the divide and heightening the alienation.[15]

In his letter to the Romans, Paul made an important connection between conflict, the devil and prayer:

> I urge you, brothers and sisters, to watch out for those who cause divisions and put obstacles in your way that are contrary to the teaching you have learned. Keep away from them. . . . By smooth talk and flattery they deceive the minds of naive people. . . . I want you to be wise about what is good, and innocent about what is evil. The God of peace will soon crush Satan under your feet. (Romans 16:17-20)

Paul had discerned Satan behind the false teaching and divisions in the church at Rome. So he exhorted them to beware of these divisive leaders and prayed that the God of Peace would crush Satan under their feet. The God of Peace uses obedient, prayerful peacemakers to crush Satan's divisive work.

So let's wage peace by resisting the devil through prayer: "Resist the devil, and he will flee from you" (James 4:7; see also 1 Peter 5:8-11). Remember, every time we pray "Your kingdom come" we are praying that God will establish his kingdom of peace and overthrow Satan's kingdom.

Here is a practical prayer to pray when you enter into conflict resolution: "God, may your peace rule in my heart. May your peace prepare the heart of the one with whom I have a conflict. May your kingdom of peace overcome the kingdom of darkness and division. Amen."

PURSUING PEACE MEANS PURSUING HARMONY

Jesus' brand of peacemaking is extensive. It embraces the breadth of humanity. But peacemaking is also intensive. The commands to love and pursue peace challenge us not only to resolve conflict but also to build accord, to humbly seek to rebuild trust and to make love deposits (or relational investments). To pursue peace is to work for in-depth harmony in the relationship.

There are many little practical ways to restore or build harmony. If we are seeking to restore harmony after marital conflict, we might give our spouse flowers or a card. We might want to invite her to talk or make him a meal.

When our daughters were in elementary school, they had their unique way of making sure my wife and I made up after a heated conversation with each other. Even though we tried hard to keep our arguments out of their hearing, they could sense the tension between us. So they folded paper into the shape of airplanes with the message "Please don't fight" printed on the wings. They would then open the door to our bedroom, where we were having our argument, fly the airplane into the room and quietly close the door and go away. The laughter that always ensued after the flight of the airplane would often bring perspective and relief. Humor is a good antidote for much of our smaller conflicts.

Harmony can be restored through sensitivity to a person's love language. According to Gary Chapman, there are five different ways people prefer to receive love: words of affirmation, acts of service, receiving gifts, quality time and physical touch.[16] The wise person learns the love language of his or her spouse, children, friends and coworkers.

For example, as a gesture of love and harmony early in my marriage, I would bring Fran flowers. I thought I was so cool. It turned out that her love language was "acts of service," so the flowers were nice but not quite hitting the mark. I needed to find other ways to restore harmony and show her love; for her, that meant doing little things around the house.

Sometimes rebuilding a relationship is very difficult. When I was younger, I would often bump heads with a person on my job. Even though we both asked for forgiveness and granted forgiveness, our relationship remained rocky. How could I pursue peace and build harmony? This is what I did: I wrote Philippians 4:8 on one side of a card: "Finally, brothers and sisters, whatever is true, whatever is noble, whatever is right, whatever is pure, whatever is lovely, whatever is admirable—if anything is excellent or praiseworthy—think about such things." On the other side, I made a list of everything positive about this person. I kept the card in my back pocket, and when I struggled with my coworker or when I was going to have an interaction with him, I pulled out the card, read both sides and prayed. This helped me restore harmony in that relationship.

4

WHAT PEACE CATALYSTS DO

PART TWO: FIVE PILLARS OF PEACEMAKING

There is no more Godlike work to be done in this world than peacemaking.

JOHN BROADUS

A church in California invited me to put on a peacemaking seminar and to speak at their Sunday services. Several months after I confirmed, they they asked me whether I would be willing to speak to elementary school–age children at their Christian school. I don't usually speak to children and wasn't too excited about it. But when I remembered how Jesus had rebuked his disciples for not receiving and blessing children, I knew I had to speak.

I wanted to get the kids' attention, so I began with a bang. "Okay, kids," I shouted. "What do football players do?" They yelled back, "Play football!" "What do baseball players do?" "Play baseball!" "What do actors do?" "Act!" Then I paused and yelled, "What do God's children do?" There was an awkward pause, then one child said, "Pray to Jesus?"

I exclaimed, "Jesus said, 'Blessed are the peacemakers, for they shall be called children of God.' God's children make peace."

"So what do God's children do?" I repeated. "Make peace!" the children yelled.

So what is the essence of making peace? I summarize it in five pillars.

FIVE PILLARS OF INTERPERSONAL PEACEMAKING

We have listed eight peacemaking pillars—or practices—in our diagram: pray for peace, pursue peace with all, take responsibility, lovingly reprove, accept reproof, ask for forgiveness, forgive others and love your enemies. So far we have looked at two of these pillars. Praying for peace provides the *power* to make peace. Pursuing peace with everyone reminds us of the *scope* of our peacemaking. And as we will learn, loving our enemies describes the *motivation* for our peacemaking.

But five of these eight pillars can be described as the essential practices of resolving conflict and restoring harmony in relationships. They are at the heart of all peacemaking.[1] In other words, they outline the concrete steps necessary for reconciliation:

- Take responsibility.
- Lovingly reprove.
- Accept reproof.
- Ask for forgiveness.
- Forgive others.

TAKE RESPONSIBILITY

When I say to take responsibility in conflict, I mean two things: be accountable and take initiative. Jesus said,

> Why do you look at the speck of sawdust in someone else's eye and pay no attention to the plank in your own eye? How can you say, "Let me take the speck out of your eye," when all the time

> there is a plank in your own eye? You hypocrite, first take the plank out of your own eye, and then you will see clearly to remove the speck from the other person's eye. (Matthew 7:3-5)

Notice the priorities Jesus gave us regarding conflict resolution: he commanded us *first* to get the plank out of our own eyes. *Then* we can move on to loving reproof (remove the speck from the other person's eye). But we need to deal with our own stuff first. We are accountable for our part in the conflict. We take responsibility for our own actions before we focus on what the other person did.

Jesus' command challenges our natural tendencies. When we face conflict, our primal response is either fight or flight. We want to attack the person verbally or to withdraw physically from the relationship. And if we decide to fight, what is our usual mode? Blame shifting and finger pointing. Just like our first parents, Adam and Eve, we blame the other rather than take responsibility (Genesis 3:11-13). So how do we overcome these tendencies? We remove the plank from our eye *first*. Even if we believe the other party is 90 percent wrong, we are still responsible for our 10 percent.

In practice, plank removal involves an *upward* and an *inward* look. Even if it seems that the other person is the only one at fault, we need to take time to humble ourselves before the Lord in prayer (the upward look). We ask him to search our hearts for sin (the inward look) before attempting to reconcile with someone else. Psalm 139:23-24 is a great Scripture to pray: "Search me, God, and know my heart; test me and know my anxious thoughts. See if there is any offensive way in me, and lead me in the way everlasting."

If we deal with our own stuff first, the odds of successfully reconciling are much higher. When I get in a conflict with Fran, I often clam up for fear that I will say something hurtful or mean. I have to step away from the tension so I can get perspective. I need a time of silence to think and pray, usually as I go about the normal tasks of life. Invariably God points out my bad attitude or unloving words that caused the conflict.

Once God gives me light about my specific failures, I reengage by asking her for forgiveness about what I did wrong. This conciliatory gesture on my part normally softens her heart. She not only forgives me but usually apologizes for her part in the conflict as well.

It is easy to see the value of these commands when others are in the process of confronting me. I like it when they humble themselves before God and search their hearts before talking to me about my issues. But why is it good for me to get the plank out of my eye if I am the one who has been sinned against? A little humility goes a long way in resolving conflict. If we don't humble ourselves before God and search our own hearts first, we remain both blind to and bound by our sin. We can never walk in freedom and integrity if we do not get the plank out of our own eye.

Taking responsibility also means taking *initiative*. Jesus repeatedly commands us "go and be reconciled," and "go and point out the fault" (Matthew 5:23-24; 18:15-17). Whether we have been offended or have hurt someone else, Jesus commands us to take the first step toward reconciliation. We are called to be proactive. The responsibility for taking steps toward peace always rests on us. Jesus says that even if the person has something against you, you still need to go to her: "Therefore, if you are offering your gift at the altar and there remember that your brother or sister has something against you, leave your gift there in front of the altar. First go and be reconciled to that person" (Matthew 5:23-24).

This essential step to conflict resolution has profound practical relevance for global conflict and foreign policy as well. Glen Stassen's groundbreaking book *Just Peacemaking* outlines ten practices for abolishing war.[2] The second practice in the book says we need to "take independent initiatives to reduce threat."[3]

> A positive theology of peace is not simply reactive, but proactive. It takes initiatives. It creates peace. It sees peace not as something to be achieved merely by refraining from war, but by taking

> peacemaking initiatives. Peace, like war, must be waged. It must be waged courageously, persistently, creatively, with imagination, heart, and wisdom.[4]

The fight-or-flight mechanism is usually our default mode in conflict. We seek to ensure our well-being by avoiding contact with our offenders, or we find ways to defeat them. In the heat of an argument, people often either want to pull a power play (fight) or to walk away (flight). But Jesus calls us to a third way.

LOVINGLY REPROVE

We neither distance ourselves from offenders nor do we attack them. Instead we tell them how they hurt us, where we think they were wrong or where we think they caused conflict. The Bible calls this "reproving" or "rebuking," something Jesus repeatedly commands us to do. For example,

> So watch yourselves. If a brother or sister sins against you, rebuke them; and if they repent, forgive them. (Luke 17:3)

> If your brother sins, go and show him his fault in private; if he listens to you, you have won your brother. (Matthew 18:15 NASB)

Reproving someone requires courage to speak difficult words. It involves being emotionally honest about ways someone has hurt us or others. But we do this in such a way as to resolve the conflict and restore the relationship.

The goal of reproof is not to prove that we are right and the other person wrong. The goal is reconciliation. Because of this, we don't just reprove the offender. We "lovingly" reprove him.

It is often said that honesty is the best policy. But honesty alone is not Jesus' policy. How we communicate is also important. We don't attack the person; we attack the problem. We are to speak the truth in love (Ephesians 4:15). Both truth and love are important. Jesus models this for us in the book of Revelation: "Those whom I love I rebuke and discipline. So be earnest, and repent" (3:19). Jesus' rebuke comes from a heart of love. Ours must too.

Paul captured the loving nature of reproof in Galatians 6:1: "Dear brothers and sisters, if another believer is overcome by some sin, you who are godly should gently and humbly help that person back onto the right path. And be careful not to fall into the same temptation yourself" (NLT).

Peacemakers understand that God is concerned about both *what* we say and *how* we say it. So how do we do this practically? Here are seven steps that will help you lovingly reprove. (Go to appendix B, a detailed description of these seven steps, when you face conflict.)

- Prepare your heart.
- Prepare your words.
- Find the right time and place.
- Stick to the facts.
- Focus on the problem, not the person.
- Invite the person to respond.
- End with resolution.

ACCEPT REPROOF

Whenever I teach on peacemaking, I ask those at the seminar, "Which aspect of conflict resolution is most difficult for you?" Invariably the most hands go up when I mention "accepting reproof." People find it hard to reprove lovingly but even harder to accept reproof.

Jesus talked about the importance of listening to a rebuke:

> If a brother or sister sins, go and point out the fault, just between the two of you. If they listen to you, you have won them over. But if they will not listen, take one or two others along, so that "every matter may be established by the testimony of two or three witnesses." If they still refuse to listen, tell it to the church;

> and if they refuse to listen even to the church, treat them as you would a pagan or a tax collector. (Matthew 18:15-17)

Four times in this famous passage about conflict resolution in the church, the word *listen* was used. The original sin may have been the cause for reproof in the first place, but Jesus taught that rejecting counsel is an even bigger sin. Learning to accept reproof is no minor issue.

The book of Proverbs says a person who rejects the advice or counsel of others is a fool. By contrast, the wise person receives reproof:

- "Whoever loves discipline loves knowledge, but whoever hates correction is stupid" (Proverbs 12:1).
- "The way of fools seems right to them, but the wise listen to advice" (Proverbs 12:15).
- "Whoever heeds life-giving correction will be at home among the wise" (Proverbs 15:31).
- "Listen to advice and accept discipline, and at the end you will be counted among the wise" (Proverbs 19:20).

Fran has done a good job coaching me about how to accept reproof. She has often participated with me in leadership meetings and has taken careful note of my responses to criticism or reproof. For example, she noticed that I would tend to lean back in my chair and cross my arms when someone challenged or rebuked me. Now when someone starts reproving me, I say to myself, *Rick, you are being confronted. Lean forward in your chair, listen with discernment, and do not cross your arms. Try to find the valid critiques in what you are hearing, and get ready to repent.*

Accepting reproof requires humility. We need to learn to be softhearted and thick-skinned—that is, receptive to counsel but not easily offended. We need to refrain from defending ourselves and to take time to consider the other person's words honestly.

Here are two practical ways you can grow in accepting reproof. First, when you are being confronted by someone, ask God to give you ears to hear where you have contributed to the problem. You may be accused of 100 percent of the problem, though you believe you are only 20 percent responsible. Take ownership of your part, and repent of what you can honestly repent of. Even if this doesn't fully satisfy the other person, it is an important conciliatory gesture. It will often soften the heart of the one confronting you and make reconciliation more possible. Remember, the goal is not to fix blame but to reconcile.

A second practical way to listen to reproof is to repeat back to the person what you heard her saying to you: "So, what I hear you saying about me is ______. Is that right?"

Accepting reproof is hard, but the one who listens to life-giving reproof lives in peace with his or her community.

ASK FOR FORGIVENESS

During a mediation session, Ron said, "Jim, you are our leader, and yet you don't deal with conflict. Your broken relationship with John has gone on too long. It has a negative impact on the whole ministry. Please get right with John."

Jim looked down and answered sheepishly, "I'm sorry."

The team wasn't satisfied with Jim's response. I wasn't either.

Later I got Jim and John together to see if I could help them resolve their conflict. In our first meeting, there was no progress. They blamed each other. They only saw the plank in the other person's eye, not their own. So I ended the meeting.

Then I got Jim and the team together again. The same scenario repeated itself. The team pleaded with Jim to repent. He meekly and pathetically said again, "I'm sorry." He didn't take responsibility for his wrongdoing, nor did he ask for forgiveness. So I took Jim aside after the meeting to coach him about making an apology. The following are some of the things I shared with him.

Asking for forgiveness is humbling. Who *likes* to admit they're wrong? But if we want to make things right, we need to do it right.

When we do ask for forgiveness, we often do it poorly. Here's a common attempt at apology: "I'm sorry that you feel that way." There are two things wrong with this apology. First, saying "I'm sorry" is not enough. Jesus talks about forgiveness, not simply feeling sorry. There is a big difference between the two. Second, by focusing on others' feelings, we are essentially blaming them for the way they feel, as though it were their problem, not ours.

Feeling sorry merely describes the state of our emotions. And let's be honest; we can be sorry for the wrong reason. Many feel sorry because their wrongdoing makes them look bad. They are more concerned about how they look than about the broken relationship. They are more concerned about guarding their reputation than about seeking reconciliation.

So how do we ask for forgiveness? The same way we ask for forgiveness from God—through confession of specific sin:

> If we confess our sins, he is faithful and just and will forgive us our sins and purify us from all unrighteousness. (1 John 1:9)

> Those who conceal their sins do not prosper, but those who confess and renounce them find mercy. (Proverbs 28:13)

There are two scriptural confessions that further clarify how we ask for forgiveness. The first comes from the story of Joseph, the other from the story of the prodigal son. Both emphasize their wrongdoing in their confession.

> I ask you to forgive your brothers the sins and the wrongs they committed in treating you so badly. (Genesis 50:17)

> Father, I have sinned against heaven and against you. I am no longer worthy to be called your son; make me like one of your hired servants. (Luke 15:18-19)

So, to ask for forgiveness means we confess the wrongdoing that caused the conflict, invite the other person to respond and ask for pardon. It means we acknowledge what we have done wrong *specifi-*

cally. We say, "I was wrong to ________," naming the specific offense. Then we follow up by asking if the person wants to talk about how our actions or words impacted her.

This is when we must stop talking. This is even harder for us than naming our wrong, because it means we must listen to how our actions have affected the other person. In naming my sin, I remain in control. And frankly, it even makes me look good: Look at me, I'm repenting! When I listen to someone I love or respect list more of my shortcomings than I first admitted, I am humbled.

The art of asking for forgiveness demands listening. We need to give the other person a chance to forgive us, to ask us questions or to share his pain about the conflict. We need to listen empathically so we can feel how our wrongdoing hurt the other person. If he refuses to talk about it, we must accept that. We cannot force reconciliation.

Finally, we humbly ask to be forgiven: "I was wrong to ________. Will you forgive me?" I get a lot of practice asking for forgiveness, so here's another thing I have learned the hard way: Ask for forgiveness, don't demand it. It is a humble request, not a command.

Many times when I asked my daughters for forgiveness, it came across as a command. Part of this was due to the power differential between us. I am the parent, the one in authority, so they felt pressured to forgive, whether they wanted to or not. Eventually I learned that I needed to give them time to forgive me. And the same was true of Fran. It may take time for the one offended to take us at our word and to trust us again.

If we are serious about true intimacy with others, we may want to ask them if we have hurt them in other ways. We can also ask if there is something we can do to make restitution or show the sincerity of our apology. We need to show the fruit of repentance (Luke 3:8). For example, my friend Cody struggled with pornography. Tensions arose when his wife, Joan, discovered his secret. He apologized and told her he would stop. But he didn't. Several years later, Joan found out that he had persisted in watching pornography. She said, "Your apologies are meaningless. If you truly love me and are sincere about your repentance, you need to get help." Cody finally got to the point where he was serious about changing. He has walked in freedom for the last fifteen years.

One final tip: do not ask for forgiveness and then give an excuse for your behavior. For example, do not say, "I was wrong and I realize I hurt you, but I have been facing so much stress recently." Making excuses for our wrongdoing negates the sincerity of our request for forgiveness, even if our excuse is justifiable.[5]

FORGIVE OTHERS

We are social beings built for peace. Every human being inherently longs for harmonious relationships. But there is a gap between our longings and how we live. That's why understanding forgiveness is so important.

The first book in the Bible begins and ends with family conflict. Genesis commences with conflict: Cain brutally murders Abel. Genesis concludes with conflict: the sons of Jacob hate their brother Joseph and sell him into slavery. One story ends in ruin, the other in reconciliation. What made the difference? Forgiveness.

The story of Joseph provides the formal introduction to forgiveness in the Bible (Genesis 37–50).[6] Joseph was the precocious "golden child"—the favorite son of his father, Jacob. Because of this his brothers "hated him and could not speak a kind word to him" (Genesis 37:4). The Hebrew word translated as "kind" in this passage is *shalom*. What was the result of the conflict between Joseph and his brothers? There was no shalom in the home.

Two God-inspired dreams got Joseph into even more trouble. He dreamt that his family would one day bow down to him. His brothers hated him even more because of this and sold him into slavery.

So Joseph spent over a decade suffering as a slave. He had plenty of time to grow bitter and harbor resentment toward his brothers. But in the midst of his trials, God was with him. In a dramatic turn of events, Joseph the dreamer became the interpreter of dreams; God showed him the interpretation of Pharaoh's dream: there would be a time of abundance followed by a devastating famine. This led to Joseph's appointment as second in command in all of Egypt under Pharaoh. He prepared Egypt for the severe famine by storing up grain during the time of plenty to prepare for the time of scarcity.

Joseph's family began to suffer during the famine, so Jacob sent his sons to acquire food for their survival. Joseph recognized his brothers when they arrived, but they did not recognize him. In fulfillment of Joseph's original dreams, his brothers bowed down to him as they requested food.

Joseph did not reveal himself to his brothers at first. Instead he tested them and toyed with them a number of times. But during the dynamic interplay between Joseph and his brothers, there was a common refrain: Joseph wept. Repeatedly.[7] Even before he revealed himself to his brothers. (I must confess, virtually every time I read of Joseph's encounter with his family, I cry. Reconciliation is awesome.)

Finally, during an emotionally charged moment, Joseph sent out all his Egyptian attendants and cried out: "I am Joseph! Is my father still living?" And "he wept so loudly that the Egyptians heard him" (Genesis 45:1-3). The brothers were terrified.

But Joseph comforted them:

> Do not be distressed and do not be angry with yourselves for selling me here, because it was to save lives that God sent me ahead of you. . . . God sent me ahead of you . . . to save your lives by a great deliverance. . . . Now hurry back to my father and say to him, . . . "God has made me lord of all Egypt. Come down to me; don't delay." . . . And he kissed all his brothers and wept over them. (Genesis 45:5, 7, 9, 15)

One reason Joseph did not hold a grudge and was able to forgive his brothers is that he believed that God was sovereignly working out his purposes. This truth fortified his ability to forgive. In spite of his pain, Joseph was able to pardon because he believed in divine providence.

When Jacob arrived in Egypt, another tearful reunion ensued. Then Joseph settled his family in the land of Goshen, where they took care of Pharaoh's livestock. When Jacob died, Joseph's brothers feared reprisal. "What if Joseph holds a grudge against us and pays us back for all the wrongs we did to him?" Joseph tearfully assured them of his forgiveness:

> "Don't be afraid. . . . You intended to harm me, but God intended it for good to accomplish what is now being done, the saving of many lives. So then, don't be afraid. I will provide for you and your children." And he reassured them and spoke kindly to them. (Genesis 50:15, 19-21)

This sad story of sibling rivalry had a happy ending, because Joseph saw the hand of God in the glove of circumstances. He understood what Paul taught later: "And we know that God causes everything to work together for the good of those who love God and are called according to his purpose for them" (Romans 8:28 NLT).

The story of Joseph is one of the most poignant examples of forgiveness in Scripture. He experienced hatred, jealousy and betrayal of the worst kind—in his family. Yet he forgave his brothers from the heart. Joseph "understood the necessity of forgiveness in closing the door on a painful past in order to open a door to a promising future."[8] Through forgiving his brothers, Joseph established shalom in the home.

But what happens if we don't forgive? Brian Zahnd reminds us that "the toxic memory of the unforgiven past poisons the present and contaminates the future."[9] Holding grudges and failing to forgive not only poisons the present, it can also harm us physically.

As a young pastor, I wanted to pray for Jean, who had been sick in bed for about a week. So I took Mike, a fellow leader in the church, with me to her home. Her husband, Jim, greeted us at the door and invited us into their bedroom. Jean had been bedridden for days and was barely able to talk. She looked miserable.

We began praying fervently for God's healing. We pleaded with God to restore her health. Suddenly, after a few minutes of prayer . . . nothing happened. Jean looked as bad as ever. But we were determined, so we continued to pray. Again nothing. Finally we waited in silence before the Lord. I sensed the Lord saying that Jean harbored unforgiveness in her heart.

So I kneeled beside the bed and said, "Jean, do you need to forgive someone for hurting you? Are you holding a grudge?" Jean's eyes got wet with tears. I encouraged her to confess her sins before the Lord and to make amends with the person who sinned against her. With a quiet, raspy voice she began to confess her sin and promised to forgive the person who hurt her. Within minutes, her countenance changed dramatically. She got out of bed and washed her face; then together we rejoiced over God's forgiveness and healing.

This reminds me of what Jesus' younger brother James says about healing and forgiveness: "Is anyone among you sick? Let them call the elders of the church to pray over them and anoint them with oil in the name of the Lord. And the prayer offered in faith will make them well; the Lord will raise them up. If they have sinned, they will be forgiven. Therefore confess your sins to each other and pray for each other so that you may be healed" (James 5:14-16).

How can we recover from the insults and injuries of our past? How can we be healed of wounds that harm our hearts and stab our souls? How can we learn to forgive like Joseph forgave his brothers? We need to learn the healing art of forgiveness. Like Joseph, we need a sovereign mindset. We need to learn how to trust in God's almighty power and loving providence in our lives. For God is ultimately in control.[10] This mindset goes a long way in helping us forgive others. But we have a huge advantage over Joseph. We live in a post-Jesus world. We see how Jesus' accepting love reaches out to the forgotten, the broken and the wounded of society. We see Jesus model and mediate forgiveness—even toward his enemies. And he expects the same from his followers.

In fact, forgiveness is the heart of the gospel and a central theme of social ethics in the New Testament. The following verses teach us three important lessons about forgiveness.

> Be kind and compassionate to one another, forgiving each other, just as in Christ God forgave you. (Ephesians 4:32)
>
> Bear with each other and forgive one another if any of you has a grievance against someone. Forgive as the Lord forgave you. (Colossians 3:13)
>
> For if you forgive others when they sin against you, your heavenly Father will also forgive you. But if you do not forgive others their sins, your Father will not forgive your sins. (Matthew 6:14-15)
>
> This is how my heavenly Father will treat each of you unless you forgive a brother or sister from your heart. (Matthew 18:35)

1. We forgive because God first forgave us. Paul's exhortations in Ephesians and Colossians indicate that Christ's prior forgiveness becomes the motive or rationale for our forgiveness. In other words, our capacity to forgive is directly related to our grasp of the gospel. As recipients of the infinite love of God in Christ, we have an infinite capacity to forgive. We forgive because God first forgave us.

2. We cannot expect God to forgive us if we do not forgive others. Jesus' words are disturbing and appear to be *un*evangelical. It seems that Jesus is teaching salvation by works. But he's not. He is teaching that our ability to forgive others is proof of our salvation. It shows that we have truly repented. According to Jesus, those who experience divine forgiveness will forgive others.

3. Forgiveness is both a choice and an emotion. It is hard to forgive. The deeper the wound, the harder it is. We are commanded not only to forgive but to forgive *from the heart* (Matthew 18:35). Jesus repeatedly stresses the importance of the heart in our relationship with him and others (Matthew 5:8, 28; 6:21; 12:34; 15:8).

Scripture indicates that forgiveness is both *volitional* and *emotional.*

We are commanded to forgive, which means that we must engage our wills and choose to obey. We are commanded to forgive from the heart, which means forgiveness involves our feelings. Thus forgiveness is one act with two dimensions. It is both a choice and an emotion. It is both an act of the will and a response from the heart.

In practice, however, our emotions usually follow our choices. It often takes time for our feelings to catch up with our decision to forgive. When a person has experienced abuse or been grievously sinned against, it may take much counseling and inner healing for forgiveness to come from the heart. But this remains Jesus' stated goal.

CULTIVATING THE HABIT OF FORGIVENESS

Rain turned to hail as Rory and Linda Brannum drove down the road. They were shocked to see a naked woman in the distance on the side of the road. As they got closer, Lashunda Richardson dove right in front of their car. Rory slammed on the brakes and screeched to a halt—barely missing her. He jumped out of the car and called 911, thinking this was a suicide attempt.

Lashunda dashed back into a parking garage on the side of the road, where her clothes were crumpled on the ground. Linda approached her cautiously, realizing something was terribly wrong with her and thinking she was perhaps a victim of a crime.

"What's going on? Can I help you?" asked Linda.

"You can help me with this!" snarled Lashunda in a cold, menacing tone as she pulled out a knife with a five-inch blade and began stabbing Linda. Linda rolled up into a fetal position to protect herself. Once Rory realized what was happening, he punched Lashunda in the face, dislodging the knife. A bystander then tackled Lashunda, who quickly jumped up and ran off.

Rory held Linda in his arms, fearing she was going to bleed to death. Another bystander kneeled down, took off her blouse and pressed it firmly into Linda's hemorrhaging wounds to stop the bleeding. The police chased Lashunda down and handcuffed her. When they put her in the police car, the hysterical woman turned around in the seat and kicked out the back window.

At the criminal trial two years later, after giving her testimony, Linda asked the judge if she could address her attacker. Linda approached Lashunda and in front of a stunned courtroom said, "I forgive you for hurting me." Lashunda, who had expressed no remorse until that point, started to cry. She was later acquitted by reason of temporary insanity.

When I interviewed Linda, she told me it was easy to forgive her assailant. "Why do you think it was easy for you?" I asked.

"I have always experienced such a strong sense of God's grace in my life. Jesus has forgiven me, so I feel compelled to forgive others," she said. "I actually care about Lashunda. I understand that there are people who have experienced much greater hurts than I have. But no one has experienced the kind of hurt that Jesus experienced. He faced terrible rejection and even God's judgment on my behalf. Christ experienced this so that we could know the forgiveness of God."

Linda continued: "Ephesians 4:32 explains my experience: 'Be kind and compassionate to one another, forgiving each other, just as in Christ God forgave you.' I realize I am not the judge. Vengeance is mine, says the Lord! *He* will repay" (see Romans 12:19).

These are two of the basic reasons for forgiveness in the Bible, so her word didn't surprise me. But the next words out of her mouth did. "I think forgiveness is related to what Jesus said: 'If you are faithful in little things, you will be faithful in large ones' [see Luke 16:10]. I always focus on forgiving little things, every single day. Because of this, I think I was able to forgive the big thing. I could forgive Lashunda because I have developed the habit of forgiving others." What a profound insight! Linda had learned the craft of forgiveness. She had cultivated the habits of making peace. She had mastered the ongoing and ever-deepening process of forgiving people from the heart.[11]

So, what does it mean to forgive someone? In its simplest terms, to forgive is to "surrender our right to get even."[12] Practically, this involves four promises:

- I will no longer dwell on this incident.
- I will not bring up this incident again or use it against you.
- I will not talk to others about this incident.
- I will not allow this incident to stand between us or hinder our relationship.[13]

We often hear that a picture is worth a thousand words. Sometimes a parable is with worth a thousand biblical commands or theological propositions.

> Therefore, the Kingdom of Heaven can be compared to a king who decided to bring his accounts up to date with servants who had borrowed money from him. In the process, one of his debtors was brought in who owed him millions of dollars. He couldn't pay, so his master ordered that he be sold—along with his wife, his children, and everything he owned—to pay the debt. But the man fell down before his master and begged him, "Please, be patient with me, and I will pay it all." Then his master was filled with pity for him, and he released him and forgave his debt. But when the man left the king, he went to a fellow servant who owed him a few thousand dollars. He grabbed him by the throat and demanded instant payment. His fellow servant fell down before him and begged for a little more time. "Be patient with me, and I will pay it," he pleaded. But his creditor wouldn't wait. He had the man arrested and put in prison until the debt could be paid in full. When some of the other servants saw this, they were very upset. They went to the king and told him everything that had happened. Then the king called in the man he had forgiven and said, "You evil servant! I forgave you that tremendous debt because you pleaded with me. Shouldn't you have mercy on

> your fellow servant, just as I had mercy on you?" Then the angry king sent the man to prison to be tortured until he had paid his entire debt. That's what my heavenly Father will do to you if you refuse to forgive your brothers and sisters from your heart. (Matthew 18:23-35 NLT)

Jesus told this parable in response to a question from Peter: "Lord, how many times shall I forgive someone who sins against me? Up to seven times?"

Jesus answered, "I tell you, not seven times, but seventy-seven times" (Matthew 18:21-22).

Jewish rabbis at that time believed that forgiving someone three times was the limit, so Peter thought he was modeling amazing grace.[14] But Jesus was not encouraging Peter to get out his calculator when he faced conflict. He was calling his followers to unlimited, radical forgiveness.

The parable then portrays God's extravagant forgiveness in pardoning the millions of dollars of debt incurred by a servant. This debt was so enormous the servant would have to work over a thousand years to pay it off. But then the servant who was pardoned turned around and demanded payment from a fellow servant who owed him a debt of only a few thousand dollars. When the fellow servant couldn't make the payment, he demanded punishment instead of granting pardon.

The parable illustrates what Jesus had told his disciples previously: "If you forgive others when they sin against you, your heavenly Father will also forgive you. But if you do not forgive others their sins, your Father will not forgive your sins" (Matthew 6:14-15). Judgment awaits those who despise God's abundant forgiveness yet do not forgive their brothers or sisters from the heart. Strong words! But Jesus is not teaching salvation by works. Forgiving others doesn't save you. It merely proves that you have truly experienced forgiveness. It is proof that you truly follow Jesus.

On another occasion, Jesus said to his disciples: "So watch yourselves. If a brother or sister sins against you, rebuke them; and if they repent, forgive them. Even if they sin against you seven times in a day and seven times come back to you saying 'I repent,' you must forgive them" (Luke 17:3-4). So how did his disciples respond to this teaching on forgiveness? The same way we should. "The apostles said to the Lord, 'Increase our faith!'" (Luke 17:5). Living a life of radical forgiveness is a faith-stretching adventure.

It is hard to overstate the importance of forgiveness for peacemaking. Forgiveness sets us free from the past and wipes the slate clean. It breaks the chain of hate[15] and restores relationships. As Miroslav Volf wisely notes, "Revenge multiplies evil. Retributive justice contains evil. . . . Forgiveness overcomes evil with good."[16]

During my lifetime, one of the most dramatic illustrations of forgiveness in history took place in South Africa. Decades of brutal oppression and unspeakable atrocities were perpetrated against South African blacks by South African whites. In 1994 the walls of racial segregation, known as apartheid, fell. Nelson Mandela, an anti-apartheid activist for over forty years and a political prisoner for twenty-seven years, rose to power as the country's first black president. But rather than exacting revenge, Mandela called for forgiveness. Desmond Tutu recounted the following from Mandela's inauguration in his book aptly titled *No Future Without Forgiveness*.

> A poignant moment on that day was when Nelson Mandela arrived with his older daughter as his companion, and the various heads of the security forces, the police and the correctional services strode to his car, saluted him, and then escorted him as the head of state. It was poignant because only a few years previously he had been their prisoner and would have been considered a terrorist to have been hunted down. He invited his white jailer to attend his inauguration as an honored guest, the first of many gestures he would make in his spec-

tacular way, showing his breathtaking magnanimity and willingness to forgive.[17]

THE RELATIONSHIP BETWEEN FORGIVENESS AND JUSTICE

Followers of Christ are commanded to forgive those who sin against them. Does this also mean that we give wrongdoers a get-out-of-jail-free card? No. Forgiveness and justice are not opposites. We affirm both. For example, in the story of King David and Bathsheba, David is forgiven but faces God's justice for his acts (2 Samuel 12).

According to Gregory Jones, a more contemporary illustration "can be seen in the extraordinary action of John Paul II, who went to an Italian prison to offer forgiveness to Mehmet Ali Agca, the man who had tried to assassinate him. But the Pope did not think that his declaration 'I forgive you' meant that Agca should be released from prison."[18] So forgiveness is not legal pardon.

Suppose you are in an abusive relationship. Imagine that your husband physically abuses you or your children. Or imagine that your wife has been unfaithful multiple times. Forgiving does not mean that you let that person get away with hurting you. Forgiving does not mean that you have to stay with the person. Nor does forgiving mean that you must achieve reconciliation with that person.[19]

Jesus said, "And when you stand praying, if you hold anything against anyone, forgive them, so that your Father in heaven may forgive you your sins" (Mark 11:25). He doesn't call us to reconcile in this case. He focuses on having a pure heart when praying. This involves forgiving those who have hurt us. Certainly we need to reconcile if at all possible, but even if the other person does not want to reconcile, Jesus urges us to forgive him. This is for our own good. Forgiveness helps us recover. It frees us from the plight of persistent pain and births hope for the future.

But what if the person who sinned against you has not been held accountable for the injustices she perpetrated against you? What if the wound is deep and the pain unbearable? What about people who have been physically battered, sexually abused or violently assaulted? According to Leah Coulter, forgiving evil offenders involves "a three phase process of 1) remembering and mourning; 2) holding the offender responsible; and 3) revoking revenge by transferring the debts owed to us and allowing God to avenge."[20]

Three Scriptures guide us in the healing process:

- Psalm 56:8 says, "You keep track of all my sorrows. You have collected all my tears in your bottle. You have recorded each one in your book" (NLT). God knows our pain. He knows about every wound and every grief we carry.
- Romans 12:19 says, "Beloved, never avenge yourselves, but leave room for the wrath of God; for it is written, 'Vengeance is mine, I will repay, says the Lord'" (NRSV). We leave room for God's wrath by crying out to God for justice. We revoke our right for personal vengeance, for God says, "Vengeance is mine."
- Exodus 34:7 says, God "will by no means leave the guilty unpunished" (NASB). Thus we present both our pain and the perpetrator before the God of righteous judgment and ask him to deal with this evil.

May the prophetic words of Brian Zahnd sink into our souls:

> Forgiveness is God's way of achieving peace. In fact, it is ultimately the only way of achieving peace between alienated parties. Justice alone is incapable of producing peace. The peace the Bible is interested in involves not only the cessation of hostilities but also the reconciliation of enemies. This is why . . . the followers of Christ, who are both the recipients and practitioners of radical forgiveness, should be the leading authorities on peace.[21]

PEACEMAKING AND CONFLICT STYLES

Now that we have reviewed the five essential pillars of interpersonal peacemaking, it's time to take a personal inventory. How do you handle conflict? What have you learned about conflict (whether implicitly or explicitly) from your family, school or workplace?

In my peacemaking journey, I have noted at least three different peacemaking styles, which I call the prophet, the pastor and the mercy show-er. These different styles emerge because of different personalities, different spiritual gifts and different life experiences. In other words, I attribute these differences to both nature and nurture.

I call them peacemaking styles, because they are the general ways different kinds of people respond to conflict. This doesn't mean people can't change, grow or use other styles. It's just that they have a preferred approach, or a default orientation, to handling conflict.

The *prophet* is a conflict exposer. This kind of person wants to get the issues on the table. Now! His or her burden is to walk in the light: "Live as children of light. . . . Have nothing to do with the fruitless deeds of darkness, but rather expose them" (Ephesians 5:8, 11).

Every peacemaking style has its strengths and weaknesses. We need conflict exposers—especially when the individual, team or community sweeps its problems under the rug. But if people with this personality type are not walking in the Spirit, they can be polarizing personalities—sometimes making things worse.

The *pastor* is a conflict controller. Pastor types do not want to address a conflict until they discern how they will actually handle it. Their burden is to walk in wisdom:

> A person finds joy in giving an apt reply—and how good is a timely word! (Proverbs 15:23)

> When there are many words, transgression is unavoidable,
> But he who restrains his lips is wise. (Proverbs 10:19 NASB)

> But the wisdom that comes from heaven is first of all pure; then peace-loving, considerate, submissive, full of mercy and good

> fruit, impartial and sincere. (James 3:17)

We need pastor types to guide us in the timing and wording of conflict. But if they are not walking in the Spirit, they can manipulate situations rather than resolve conflict.

The burden of *mercy show-ers* is that they and others walk in grace:

> A person's wisdom yields patience; it is to one's glory to overlook an offense. (Proverbs 19:11)

> Above all, love each other deeply, because love covers over a multitude of sins. (1 Peter 4:8)

As these verses teach, certain conflicts are unnecessary. But if mercy show-ers are not walking in the Spirit, they can minimize sin and act as peacekeepers rather than peacemakers.

Let me illustrate how these styles work in real life. One of my mentors, Greg Livingstone, is a prophet, so he loves to get the issues on the table. He has exhorted me many times in the past to confront certain issues. As a pastor type, I once responded, "And what do you propose I do once the issues are exposed?"

Greg laughed and said, "I am not sure!"

I assured him I was praying and thinking about how to handle the issue. And I did once I discerned the appropriate responses.

I remember counseling a husband and wife who copastored a church. She was a prophet and he was a mercy show-er. (I think you can see where this is going.) As I asked questions about the conflict they faced in the church, tears welled up in the wife's eyes. Other leaders in the church were criticizing her, but her husband, as a conflict avoider, had ignored the issue. I exhorted him to go against the grain of his temperament and speak to the other leaders. I am happy to say that he received my reproof and confronted the situation. And there has been a profound turnaround in the church.

Why is it important to understand these styles? Because our natural tendency has strengths and weaknesses. We need to know when to act according to our strength and when to approach conflict with a different style. So knowing one another's peacemaking styles on a team enhances communication and team dynamics. Each style needs to appreciate its own strength and the strength of others. There are certain times when prophets need to shut up, mercy show-ers need to speak up and pastors need to speed up.

These three peacemaking styles describe how people approach conflict, but they don't describe what happens during an actual conflict. For this we need to understand the *five styles of conflict*—a well-known rubric in the field of conflict resolution: competing, avoiding, compromising, accommodating and collaborating (see figure 4.1).[22]

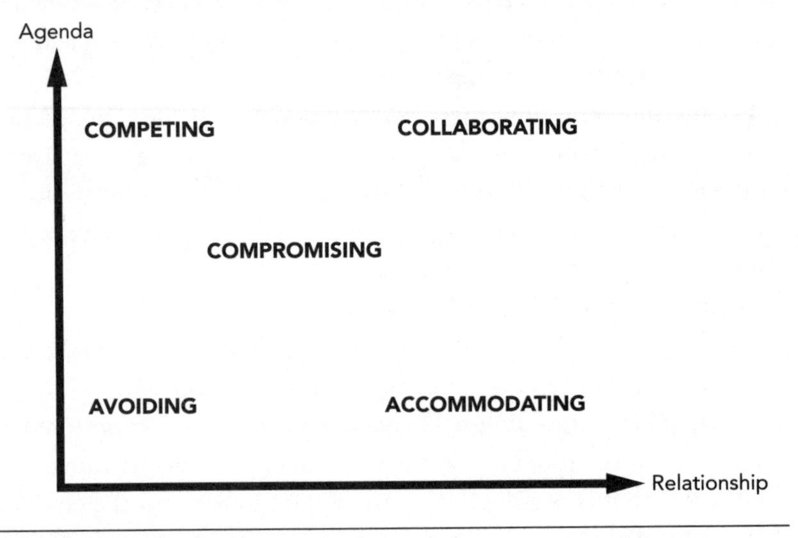

Figure 4.1. Five styles of conflict

Competing means the person puts a high focus on the agenda and a low focus on relationships. Those who compete tend to have the attitude "We're doing it my way." This is an "I win, you lose" scenario. *Avoiding* means the person puts a low focus on his or her own agenda and a low focus on relationship. The attitude is "Forget it. Conflict? What conflict?" This is an "I lose, you lose" scenario. *Compromising* means the person puts a medium focus on his or her own agenda and a medium focus on relationship. The attitude is "I'll meet you halfway." This is an "I win some and you win some" scenario. *Accommodating* means the person puts a low focus on his or her own agenda and a high focus on relationship. The attitude is "Whatever you're happy with is fine with me." This is a "you win, I lose" scenario. *Collaborating* means the person puts a high focus on her own agenda and a high focus on relationship. The attitude is "My preference is _____. Please tell me yours." This is a win-win scenario. Both parties gain.

A student raised his hand during a lecture I gave on peacemaking at the Columbus Vineyard. "Rick, is there really such thing as a win-win solution? Isn't compromise always involved in conflict resolution?"

I said, "John, good question. In many cases compromise is necessary because the parties are so emotionally charged that they can't think creatively. I suppose there is really a continuum between compromise and collaboration. One end of the continuum demands painful compromise while the other end involves satisfying collaboration. And of course there are varying degrees of compromise along the continuum. But in many cases a good mediator can help people look at their problem so differently that both sides feel like it is a win for them."[23]

Figure 4.1 can be used in a number of practical ways. First, it helps people discern their most natural approach to conflict. Second, it helps them understand the strengths and weaknesses of each style. Third, it highlights that conflict has a dual axis: concern for our agenda and concern for the relationship. Fourth, it helps people see that the goal should be collaboration.[24]

5

HOW PEACE CATALYSTS LOVE

The biblical test case for love of God is love of neighbor;
the biblical test case for love of neighbor is love of enemy.
Failure to love the enemy is failure to love God.

WAYNE NORTHEY

LOVE YOUR NEIGHBOR

My friend Jim Mullins loves to tell stories of his interactions with friends in Turkey. When the topic turned to Jesus, he would often mention Jesus' command to love enemies. He did this to highlight the uniqueness of Jesus and his teaching. His Turkish friends were deeply touched by Jesus' teaching and would ask, "Why don't more Christians in America obey this?" Ultimately Jim returned to America to help the church do just that by helping found Peace Catalyst International.

I previously described peacemaking as "love in action." Why? Because there is a huge overlap in meaning between peace and love. The first mention of "love of neighbor" in the Bible makes this clear: "Do not seek revenge or bear a grudge against anyone among your people, but love your neighbor as yourself" (Leviticus 19:18). What it is the opposite of seeking revenge or bearing a grudge, according to this verse?

Love! True love seeks right relationships by overcoming grudges. That is how love is described, and that is what peacemaking is.

A biblical understanding of love always pushes us toward peace. If we truly love others, we want to be at peace with them. Making peace, or working toward reconciliation, is an act of love demonstrated most profoundly in Jesus' life and death. So let's explore the Bible's teaching on love and ultimately what it means to love even our enemy.

Jesus told the parable of the good Samaritan in response to a religious expert's question: "Who is my neighbor?" This religious leader wanted to limit the definition of neighbor so that the demand of neighbor love remained within his comfort zone (Luke 10:29-37). Like most people of his day, he believed that *neighbor* referred to someone of his race or faith. *Neighbor* meant someone "like me" or a person "I like."

But Jesus' revolutionary parable shattered his relational categories. Jesus showed that love for neighbor reaches beyond race or religion, color or creed. The hero of the story was a despised Samaritan, after all! Samaritans were viewed as heretics—syncretistic in faith, ethnically inferior, excluded from the true worship of God (John 4:9). In other words, a "good" Samaritan would have been an oxymoron for a Jew. Yet this Samaritan showed compassion toward his enemy, the Jew, demonstrating that love of neighbor includes the people we love the least. An accurate understanding of love of neighbor means we love even our enemy.

LOVE YOUR ENEMY

Jesus' teaching about love of enemy, however, is not just taught in a parable. It is explicitly commanded.

> You have heard that it was said, "Love your neighbor and hate your enemy." But I tell you, love your enemies and pray for those who persecute you, that you may be children of your Father in

> heaven. He causes his sun to rise on the evil and the good, and sends rain on the righteous and the unrighteous. If you love those who love you, what reward will you get? Are not even the tax collectors doing that? And if you greet only your own people, what are you doing more than others? Do not even pagans do that? Be perfect, therefore, as your heavenly Father is perfect. (Matthew 5:43-48)

Many Christians think this command to love our enemies reflects an unrealistic and idealistic standard, and so they've engaged in what could be called the hermeneutics of evasion—figuring out ways to interpret it so it doesn't apply to their lives.[1] But this teaching is part of kingdom ethics in the Sermon on the Mount. We can't ignore the fact that this is Jesus' command. And it is repeated at least thirteen times in the New Testament (see, for example, Matthew 5:43-48; Luke 6:27-36; Romans 12:20-21). The number and diversity of these commands underscore their importance:

- Love your enemy (three times).
- Do not resist an evil person.
- Turn the other cheek.
- Do not withhold your coat/shirt.
- Go with them two miles (the extra mile).
- Give to everyone who asks/lend.
- Pray for those who persecute you/mistreat you.
- Do good to those who hate you (two times).
- Bless those who curse you.
- Do not demand back (what someone takes).
- Feed them.
- Give them a drink.
- Overcome evil with good.

And please note: the different commands related to love of enemy refer to *acts* of kindness, not *feelings* of kindness, so enemy love is practical and possible. This parallels the Bible's teaching on forgiveness. Enemy love begins as an act of the will. It originates with a choice and practical actions. But as we invest in the enemy, our hearts soften and our feelings change.

In the Sermon on the Mount (Matthew 5–7) and the Sermon on the Plain (Luke 6), the term *enemy* was broadly defined. Jesus' teaching indicates that an enemy could be anyone. Figure 5.1 shows the spectrum of possibilities in practice.

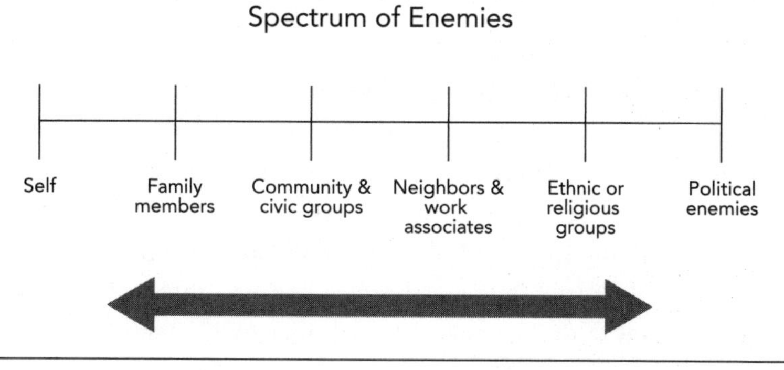

Figure 5.1

Our enemies could be terrorists who literally want to kill us, or an enemy can be the person we married who seems to be standing in the way of our cherished goals. Sometimes we are our own worst enemy. Our negative self-talk can sabotage our best intentions. No matter who our enemy is, we have the God of Peace living *in* us, who wants to love those people *through* us.

So, what does this mean practically? Love of neighbor and enemy are central peacemaking tenets. Love means we reach out to those of different races and religions, like the good Samaritan did. Love means we welcome and eat with society's outcasts, like Jesus did. Love means we engage people without fear of compromise or contamination, like

Jesus did. Love means we build a relationship with the other and even the enemy, unlike the Pharisees did.

The strong both-and nature of this radical Jesus unnerves many people. The majority of Christians contend earnestly for Jesus' exclusive truth claims. They boldly affirm, "Jesus is the way, the truth and the life" (see John 14:6) but quietly ignore his command to "love your enemy." They miss or minimize Jesus' inclusive love aims. True followers of Jesus must both declare truth and model love. To deny either truth or love is to deny Jesus.

Love pushes us beyond our comfort zone and calls us to peace with everyone. Thus peacemaking is extensive. It embraces everyone. Yes, everyone. It looks like this:

> A Turkish officer raided and looted an Armenian home. He killed the aged parents and gave the daughters to the soldiers, keeping the eldest daughter for himself. Sometime later she escaped and trained as a nurse. As time passed, she found herself nursing in a ward of Turkish officers. One night, by the light of a lantern, she saw the face of this officer. He was so gravely ill that without exceptional nursing he would die. The days passed, and he recovered. One day, the doctor stood by the bed with her and said to him, "But for her devotion to you, you would be dead." He looked at her and said, "We have met before, haven't we?" "Yes," she said, "we have met before." "Why didn't you kill me?" he asked. She replied, "I am a follower of him who said, 'Love your enemies.'"[2]

LOVE YOUR ENEMIES . . . BUT WHAT ABOUT TERRORISTS?

A salesman once asked me what I did. I explained to him that I was a peacemaker and a consultant on Christian-Muslim relations. He then said smugly, as if he were making a brilliant point, "All Muslims are not terrorists, but all terrorists are Muslims."

This common viewpoint is blatantly false. Timothy McVeigh, the

Oklahoma bomber, was not a Muslim. And what about the blond-haired, blue-eyed, self-professed Christian Anders Behring Breivik, who shocked the world by killing over ninety people in Norway in 2011. The Tamil Tigers of Sri Lanka are not Muslims. The Catholics and Protestants of Ireland are not Muslims. The Basque separatists of Spain are not Muslims.

Hating and killing in the name of God knows no religious boundaries. So let's get this straight: there are extremists among all races and all religions. And we must stand against all types of violent extremism.

I can imagine a question that might come to mind when I mention terrorism in a book on peacemaking. "Okay, Rick, how can we be true peacemakers when we face evil terrorists? These people purposely murder innocent people to make a political point. Doesn't the Bible say a lot about justice and punishing evil people?" Weighty questions demand worthy answers. To address these important questions, let's study the relationship between church and state in Romans 12–13 and answer this question: "How can we love Muslims and deal with terrorists?"

Differentiate between all Muslims and the few Muslim terrorists. First, we need a view of Muslims that is as accurate and discerning as possible. The Muslim world is radically diverse. There are over 1.5 billion Muslims, comprising about two thousand unique ethnic groups in more than fifty-two Muslim-majority nations, with large minorities in another forty countries. There are huge variations in expressions of Islam. For example, women must be fully covered in some countries, while they do not adopt a Muslim dress code in others. Women are omitted from the public sphere in some societies, while they serve as heads of state in others. There are Islamic states where government and religion are intertwined, such as Saudi Arabia and Iran, and states with a secular government, such as Turkey.

The Islamic world contains significant theological and ideological diversity as well. Islam has two major sects: Sunni, comprising 85 percent of the Muslim world, and Shia, comprising 15 percent, with eight recognized schools of Islamic jurisprudence.[3] Islamism[4] is on the rise, and, at the same time, important voices in the Muslim world are articulating an interpretation of Islam that calls for peaceful relations with non-Muslims.[5]

Sufism is a widespread mystical tendency, expressing itself through many diverse Sufi orders and organizations existing within various forms of both Sunni and Shia Islam. Some estimate that as many as 50 percent of the world's Muslims may be Sufis in the widest sense of the term.[6] The impact of Sufism on the various branches of Islam can be compared to the charismatic movement's permeation of Christianity.

In light of the great diversity mentioned above, how should we understand Muslims? How can we discern between the average Muslim and the terrorist? Colin Chapman, a well-respected British evangelical scholar of Islam, encourages us to find a middle path between demonization of Islam and naive political correctness:

> Many Christians feel that if they condemn the naivety of many secular people (and some Christians) who are willing to give in to Muslim demands/requests, the only alternative is to demonize Islam and take a hard line on every public issue related to Islam. A middle way between these two extremes would mean (a) being realistic about the real intentions of *some* Muslims, (b) recognizing the diversity among Muslims and relating to them as individuals and groups with openness and honesty, (c) taking a firm stand on issues of human rights, (d) working for the common good of the whole society, (e) demonstrating a fundamental respect for Islam without agreeing with all its teaching, and (f) unapologetically commending the Christian faith through word and deed.[7]

The Venn diagram (figure 5.2)[8] illustrates the categories and population proportion of the various types of Muslims in the world today.

Secularist Muslims reject Islam as a guiding force for their lives,

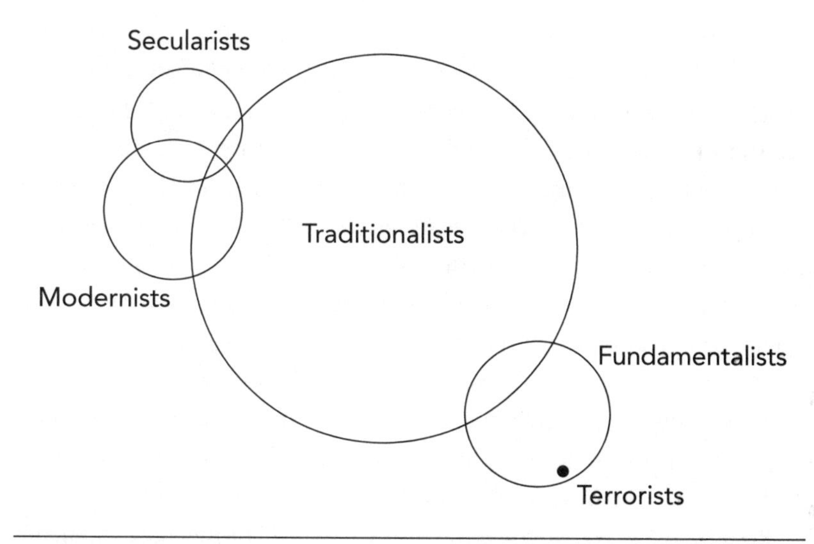

Figure 5.2. Categories of Muslims

whereas modernists have a "West is best" approach to Islam. They want to change and adapt Islam to the modern world. Traditionalists view Islam as a source and treasure that must be wisely and flexibly applied to the modern world. Fundamentalists are literalists who strive to obey the Qur'an and the Hadith while ignoring or rejecting many of the classical traditions of Islam. They seek to model their lives after Muhammad and his earliest disciples. Terrorists are militant Muslims who espouse violence to force all people to follow Shariah law.

I remember my surprise when a Muslim friend in Saudi Arabia said jubilantly, "Our government just killed those terrorists!" Why was he so happy? Most people don't realize that more Muslims have been killed by terrorists than anyone else. The majority of Muslims believe their religion has been hijacked by violent radicals. They view "Islamic" terrorists much the same way that most Christians view the infamous Westboro Baptist Church—the church with the notorious hate-mongering picketing ministry that hates Muslims, "fags" and the media.[9]

The vast majority of Muslims are just like you and me. They want to live in peace. They want a good job and a good education for their children. They want to be treated with dignity and respect.[10] Moreover, contrary to what the media might say, most prominent Muslim leaders have taken a strong and public stand against any form of terrorism.[11]

Differentiate between the role of the church and the role of the state. Flag-waving patriotism and Bible-believing faith often go hand in hand in the United States. This fusion of church and state, however, can be problematic when it comes to relating to Muslims. This is most apparent when we seek to reconcile the challenge of loving Muslims with dealing with terrorists. Fortunately, the Bible gives us wise guidance regarding these issues in Romans 12 (the role of the church) and Romans 13 (the role of the state).

Romans 13 is unequivocal regarding the role of the state: "For the one in authority is God's servant for your good. But if you do wrong, be afraid, for rulers do not bear the sword for no reason. They are God's servant, agents of wrath to bring punishment on the wrongdoer" (Romans 13:4). The state is God's servant. It bears the sword as an agent of God's wrath. The state has a God-given responsibility to promote the common good, uphold justice and protect their citizens. No love of enemy here.

So how do we reconcile what Paul taught with Jesus' call to love our enemy? We read Romans 13 in context. Paul prefaced his teaching on government by calling the church to radical peacemaking in Romans 12: "Do not repay anyone evil for evil. . . . If it is possible, as far as it depends on you, live at peace with everyone. Do not take revenge. . . . Do not be overcome by evil, but overcome evil with good" (Romans 12:17-19, 21).

After the teaching about the role of the state (Romans 13:1-7), Paul shifts back to the role of the church, with an emphasis on love. Love does no harm to neighbor and is the fulfillment of the law (Romans 13:8-10). In other words, Paul sandwiches this teaching on the role of the state with the church's call to pursue peace (Romans 12:17-21) and embody love (Romans 13:8-10).

The contrast between the role of the church and the state is staggering. Whereas Jesus' followers are called to a peacemaking ethic of sacrificial love, the state is called to bring justice. The church extends the olive branch, while the state bears the sword.

A deeper look at Romans 12–13 further highlights the radical difference between the role of the church and state. Paul describes a Christian response to evil in these chapters.[12] He uses the terms *kakos* and *poneros* (which can both translated as *evil* or *wrong*) nine times in this short section:

- "Hate what is evil; cling to what is good" (Romans 12:9).
- "Do not repay anyone evil for evil" (v. 17).
- "Do not be overcome by evil, but overcome evil with good" (v. 21).
- "For rulers are not a cause of fear for good behavior, but for evil. . . . But if you do what is evil, be afraid; for it does not bear the sword for nothing; for it is a minister of God, an avenger who brings wrath on the one who practices evil" (Romans 13:3-4 NASB).
- "Love does no wrong to a neighbor; therefore love is the fulfillment of the law" (v. 10 NASB).

Paul's reflection on evil can be summarized in five propositions:

- Evil is to be hated.
- Evil is not to be repaid.
- Evil is to be overcome with good.
- Evil is to be punished by the government.
- Evil is never to be done to a neighbor.

Propositions 1, 2, 3 and 5 describe a peacemaking ethic of sacrificial love. They reflect a nonviolent response to evil and encourage love of enemy. Nothing is said about punishing evil.[13] By contrast, proposition 4 says the government is expected to punish evil. How do we reconcile this?

As followers of Christ, we have a dual allegiance. Jesus taught that we must "render to Caesar the things that are Caesar's; and to God the things that are God's" (Matthew 22:21 NASB). Implicit in this command is the fact that the church and state have distinct roles and responsibilities. We are citizens of heaven and citizens of earth with responsibilities to both.[14]

We are called to submit to the governing authorities because they are servants of God for our good. As good citizens *and* followers of Christ, we should support our government's struggle against the evil menace of terrorism. But exactly how this finds expression varies according to a person's conscience, especially when it comes to war.

People usually fit into one of two categories. Some embrace *pacifism,* which affirms an antiwar ethic. Most pacifists believe that the use of force by police is warranted but mass killing in war is always wrong. Pacifists believe in settling disputes nonviolently.[15] *Just-war theory* affirms that war is a necessary evil at times but must meet strict criteria to be truly just. It outlines criteria for going to war and criteria for executing war in such a way as to reduce or minimize violence.[16]

A new ethics of war and peace has emerged call *just peacemaking.*[17] Pacifists and just-war theorists debate whether or not a war is justified. By contrast, just peacemaking focuses on proactively working to prevent war and spread peace. Just-peacemaking advocates have discerned ten practices based on techniques of diplomacy, conflict resolution, repentance and nonviolent action that have been empirically proven to prevent wars and end conflict. Because of its focus on preventing war, just peacemaking can be affirmed by both pacifists and just-war theorists. (See appendix E for a full summary of *just peacemaking.*)

Implicit in the teaching about government in Romans 13:1-7 is that governments are accountable to God for supporting good and punishing evil. Thus there are times we prophetically resist the state when we believe its actions contradict God's moral standards. Cases of civil disobedience like this can be found in Scripture. For example, the

Hebrew midwives feared God and refused to obey the Egyptian king's command to kill all Jewish male infants (Exodus 1:15-20). Shadrach, Meshach and Abednego refused to bow down to the golden statue of King Nebuchadnezzar (Daniel 3:9-18). And Daniel refused to obey the ordinance against praying to any god except the king (Daniel 6:6-10). In the most compelling case of civil disobedience, when the apostles were commanded not to preach about Jesus, they boldly affirmed before the religious authorities, "We must obey God rather than men" (Acts 5:29 NASB).

In 2007 I joined a group of evangelicals who spoke out against torture in the early years of the so-called war on terror. Our focus: no torture, no exceptions. I served on the advisory board of Evangelicals for Human Rights, an organization that became the New Evangelical Partnership for the Common Good.[18] And ultimately the board of the National Association of Evangelicals (which represents more than 45,000 local churches from forty different denominations) endorsed the statement "An Evangelical Declaration Against Torture: Protecting Human Rights in an Age of Terror."[19]

This declaration provides a substantial theological and political analysis of vital issues. Perhaps one statement from this lengthy document will whet your appetite to read the whole thing:

> The abominable acts of 9/11, along with the continuing threat of terrorist attacks, create profound security challenges. However, these challenges must be met within a moral and legal framework consistent with our values and laws, among which is a commitment to human rights that we as evangelicals share with many others. In this light, we renounce the resort to torture and cruel, inhuman, and degrading treatment of detainees, call for the extension of procedural protections and human rights to all detainees, seek clear government-wide embrace of the Geneva Conventions, including those articles banning torture and cruel treatment of prisoners, and urge the reversal of any U.S.

> government law, policy, or practice that violates the moral standards outlined in this declaration.[20]

In conclusion, we must distinguish between the role of the church *and* the state. As followers of Christ, we are called to pursue peace *and* embody love. As US citizens, we support *and* challenge our government. We obey both Romans 12 *and* Romans 13. We are called to love Muslims *and* deal with terrorists.

6

HOW PEACE CATALYSTS MEDIATE AND COMMUNICATE

Peacemakers who sow in peace reap a harvest of righteousness.

JAMES, THE BROTHER OF JESUS

Fran and I had enjoyed the company of our close friends, Jack and Jenny, all day. But we noticed a few times they were struggling in their relationship. They had found themselves drifting apart as they got older. The wife sensed a new calling, and so their old ways of hanging out and doing things together had changed. There were subtle and not-so-subtle tensions.

Finally, I asked them if Fran and I could facilitate mediation between them. They happily agreed. So we sat down at a table together, and I explained the ground rules: "Fran and I are merely facilitators. We are not counselors. We are here to help you communicate. We are in charge of the process, and you guys are in charge of the results."

Jack and Jenny shared their hearts with one another for over an hour. Jack talked about the way things used to be and the pain he felt because they didn't do many things together anymore. Jenny explained why she could no longer live like that. They were stuck.

Finally, Fran suggested that they look at their problem differently. "You are in a new stage of life, so you need to come up with new ways of living together. Why don't we make a list of things you could both agree to do together in the future?" They smiled and went at it. The tension in the air gave way to hope as we came up with a number of practical ways they could do life together in this new phase of their relationship.

MEDIATION FOR DUMMIES

The term *peacemaker* combines two Greek words meaning "peace" (*eirene*) and "to make, do or produce" (*poieo*). Peacemakers are literally "peace doers," implying that peacemakers step in to resolve conflict and restore harmony. Thus, the very term *peacemaker* implies mediation. The vast majority of mediation is informal—between friends, family, neighbors, schoolmates and business associates (just like we did with Jack and Jenny). The skills to negotiate and to help people navigate conflict (in other words, mediate) are, in fact, basic life skills.

Mediation refers to third-party peacemaking. To mediate is to facilitate a conversation between people at odds with one another. It is about helping them problem solve, helping them resolve conflict. I read an excellent, practical book on mediation recently and laughed when the author (a lawyer who has mediated over seven thousand cases) wrote that her ninety-year-old parents still mediate between her and her sisters.[1] Wow, a trained lawyer and veteran mediator still needed the practical help of her parents to mediate conflict with her siblings.

Scripture speaks of mediation in a number of places. For example, there were disputes at Corinth about which believers filed lawsuits against each other in secular courts (1 Corinthians 6:1-8). Paul was shocked by these unloving acts and frustrated by this negative witness to those outside the church. So he asked a pointed question: "Isn't there anyone in all the church who is wise enough to decide these issues?" (1 Corinthians 6:5 NLT). In other words, he criticized the Corinthians for not finding any mediators in their Christian community.

In Philippians 4:2-3 Paul exhorted someone he called his "true companion" to mediate between two women leaders in conflict, Euodia and Syntyche. In the book of Philemon, Paul himself mediated between Philemon and his runaway slave, Onesimus. But the most profound example of a mediator is Jesus. As Paul wrote, "There is one God and one mediator between God and human beings, Christ Jesus, himself human" (1 Timothy 2:5).

What does this statement say about Jesus in terms of the practice of mediation? In the same way Jesus was fully God and fully human, so too the mediator immerses himself or herself in the perspective of all sides of the conflict. Whether professional mediators doing formal mediation or nonprofessionals working informally, good mediators build bridges. They imitate Jesus (whether they realize it or not) in that they seek to understand and represent both sides of those who are in conflict.

The ideal of Scripture is that the two parties in conflict work things out between themselves—a cooperative resolution as shown in Matthew 18:15: "If a brother or sister sins, go and point out the fault, just between the two of you. If they listen to you, you have won them over."

But often people in conflict need help. So they turn to a trusted, neutral third party to aid them in resolving their dispute (or they should). Mediators help people do what they can't do on their own: have an honest conversation in such a way that both parties listen to one another and discern a way forward. They also help them work through the five essential pillars of peacemaking where necessary.

But it's not enough to have a trusted third party mediate. That party needs to understand and fulfill the role of a neutral third party. In 2009 I was experiencing conflict with Carl and Jim. We had some intense disagreements about the Islamic view of God, so we asked Roger to mediate our conversation over the phone. We all loved and respected Roger, so he seemed like the perfect person.

I began by explaining my viewpoint. Soon Carl and Jim went on the attack. The conversation quickly turned sour. Finally, after a number of emotionally charged theological volleys, Roger said, "Rick, I agree with Carl and Jim." Wow! Three against one. That's not supposed to happen in mediation. The mediator has a right to his opinion, but he's called to facilitate the conversation. He is not supposed to be the judge. Moral of the story: don't just choose a trusted third party to facilitate the discussion. Make sure that person understands and is committed to the neutral role of a mediator.

Mediation is both a science and an art; it is complex and multifaceted. But I want to help you actually practice mediation. So I will make this simple. Here is my attempt at "Mediation for Dummies."

As the two parties talk, mediators do four things:

- They help defuse volatile conversations with gentle words (Proverbs 15:1; James 3:13-18).
- They support conciliatory gestures.
- They reframe the problem so it is a win-win solution (also described as a both-gain approach).
- They encourage the disputants to negotiate an agreement and put it in writing.

1. Mediators help defuse volatile conversations with gentle words. Emotions are an integral part of the reconciliation process.[2] So they must be addressed if there is to be resolution. Yet they must be handled with great sensitivity. Why? Because emotions can either hinder or help resolution.

The wise mediator allows people to share their painful stories. Venting, to a certain extent, can be helpful because it gives one party the opportunity to feel the hurt of the other. Often just getting things off our chest reduces emotional tension and allows us to do problem solving. Letting off emotional steam can deescalate the intensity of the conflict if handled tactfully by the mediator.

It is the responsibility of the mediator to make sure that venting doesn't get out of hand. Too much emotion can exacerbate the conflict, increase the tension between the parties and hinder their ability to negotiate an agreement. Thus the mediator needs to *manage the emotions* during the interaction. The Scriptures show us how:

> A gentle answer turns away wrath, but a harsh word stirs up anger. (Proverbs 15:1)

> But the wisdom that comes from heaven is . . . peace-loving, considerate, . . . full of mercy and good fruit. . . . Peacemakers who sow in peace reap a harvest of righteousness. (James 3:17-18)

Just when the conflict seems to escalate emotionally, the mediator steps in with gentle words to deflect anger and to keep tempers from flaring.

*2. **Mediators support conciliatory gestures.*** Whenever someone apologizes, takes responsibility for the conflict, expresses positive feelings for the other or initiates a win-win agreement, she is making a conciliatory gesture. The mediator rewards and underscores such gestures of peace by asking questions, such as "Would you say more about that?" or "Did you notice what he just said?"

But it's tricky. Conciliatory gestures are often mixed with hostile comments. Can you find the conciliatory gesture in the following exchange? Bea says, "You know, Ty, you think you're so damn smart! You truly are a whiz as an analyst, and I could use your help a lot of times. But when you look right at me when you say words like *immoral* and *selfish* and *babies*, it just sets me off."[3]

Did you find it? In the midst of the accusation was an affirmation: "You truly are a whiz as an analyst, and I could use your help a lot of times." It is up to the mediator to interrupt the conversation and point out the conciliatory gesture: "Bea, a moment ago you complimented

Ty for being a whiz as an analyst and said you could use his help. Can you say more about that?"[4]

3. Mediators reframe the problem so it is a win-win or a both-gain solution. The mediator is in charge of the process, while the parties are in charge of the outcome. So the mediator helps them come to a cooperative resolution. And how do you help those in conflict come up with a cooperative resolution?

The mediator gets the disputants to define the problem. Typically the problem is defined or framed with exaggeration and in such a way as to cast blame. It's the mediator's job to reframe the problem so that the disputants can agree on a solution. Mayer writes, "The art of reframing is to maintain the conflict in all of its richness but to help people look at it in a more open-minded and hopeful way."[5] Here's a good example of reframing:

> Alex, a young hire at a tech company, is in a dispute with a middle manager at the company: "Chris is the most obstinate person I have ever met. I think she wants me gone so she can continue to run our division like a family, where she is the all-powerful mother, instead of like a business poised for success." The mediator stops Alex at this point and reframes the statement as follows: "It appears you feel Chris is unwilling to collaborate with you and may want you out of the company. You also seem to want her to work for the success of the business. Is that right, Alex?" Note how the mediator eliminated the toxic language of "obstinate" while still honoring the intent of the statement. Additionally, she reconstructed the last sentence by taking out the characterization of her as an "all-powerful mother" and reframed it into a focus on his desire that Chris care as he does about the success of the company.[6]

Mediators help people move from the "me against you" phase of conflict to the "us against them" phase of conciliation. They help both parties see the conflict as a mutual problem to be resolved. By reframing the problem, they enable the disputants to come to a win-win solution instead of a win-lose result. Mediators facilitate collaboration.[7]

4. Mediators encourage the disputants to negotiate an agreement and put it in writing. A written agreement should be balanced and behaviorally specific. It is balanced if both disputants see a benefit in making the deal work. It is behaviorally specific if it defines clearly who is to do what, by when, for how long and under what conditions.

Below is a sample of a negotiated agreement between two disputants.

Memo of Understanding between Jim Ellis and John Simon
Re: Future Communication
7/6/13

- If we aren't sure about what the other is saying, we will repeat back what we think he is saying to clarify or confirm.
- We realize we have different ways of processing information. So we will give the other an agreed-upon time frame necessary to reflect on the issues (for example, including a short break to reflect on it or coming back the next day).
- If conflict/differences between us persists, we will invite an agreed-upon third party early in the process to help communicate effectively.
- We give each other permission to give feedback regarding the other's communication, especially if the words, attitudes or body language are not congruent (for example, if words say one thing and body language says another).
- We will let the other know when they have hurt us by saying, "I feel hurt (disrespected, etc.) when you________."
- We give each other permission to point out when we engage in selective listening (for example, I share three points with the other and he only focuses on one point; or the other latches onto a minor point and misses the main point).

- We give each other permission to stop the other when there is gossip or when the other feels uneasy about what is being said.
- We will not judge one another's motive or intent, but give permission to clarify motives.

JAMES MEDIATES A CONFLICT
A New Testament Case Study

One of the best examples of mediation in the Bible comes from one of the most significant conflicts in the Bible—the Jerusalem Council, described in Acts 15. At stake was the essence of the gospel.

We know the outcome of this council and rejoice in the wisdom of the early church to free the gospel from its Jewish cultural moorings. But we miss valuable relational lessons if we see this only as a battle for truth. It is also a brilliant example of peacemaking and conflict resolution—facilitated by Jesus' younger brother, James.

The Jerusalem Council engaged in a serious, controversial battle for truth. There were no bad guys at this council, just two different groups who both believed they were biblical. Those who belonged to the party of the Pharisees believed the gospel was about Jesus and keeping the law (if we had been Jews living at that time, we would have been very sympathetic to their view). By contrast, Paul, Barnabas and Peter believed the gospel was about Jesus alone.

This was no lightweight debate. It was a heated controversy. Luke described the conflict with terms like "sharp dispute" and "much discussion" (Acts 15:2, 7).

The Jerusalem Council ultimately came to a strong, unified decision about what to do. Luke said there was agreement between the apostles, the elders and the whole church (Acts 15:22). He described this consensus with the memorable words "It seemed good to the Holy Spirit and to us" (Acts 15:28).

James demonstrated the wisdom and skill of a peacemaker by leading a divided Jerusalem Council into unity. The Pharisees argued from the Old Testament about the importance of circumcision and obedience to the law. By contrast, Paul, Barnabas and Peter argued from experience: God repeatedly confirmed the gospel among the Gentiles through signs and wonders. Just as God poured out His Holy Spirit on Jewish believers in Acts 2, he was now doing the same among the Gentiles.

So how did James bring those Scripture-quoting Pharisees together with those experience-focused apostles? He did what all mediators do in a heated conflict. He helped the disputants see the problem in a new way. He *reframed the problem* by quoting Scripture no one had mentioned in the conflict—an Old Testament prophecy from Amos about Gentiles becoming a people for God's name (Acts 15:14-18).

By doing this, James proposed a win-win decision. The concerns of both sides of the debate were addressed. By quoting Scripture that had not been considered, he showed agreement between the Scripture and the experience of the early church, between the witness of the prophets and the experience of the apostles.

James not only reframed the conflict, however. He also *proposed a solution* that addressed both groups. He quoted Scripture confirming apostolic experience among the Gentiles *and* concluded: "We do not trouble those who are turning to God from among the Gentiles" (Acts 15:19 NASB).

James the peacemaker focused on truth—and love. He concluded that the gospel was free from Jewish law. Salvation was by grace alone! It was about Jesus plus nothing. He suggested that obedience to four Jewish laws was necessary for the sake of fellowship between Jewish believers and Gentile believers (Acts 15:20-22); love demands that we show sensitivity to others (Romans 14:15; 1 Corinthians 13:5). Obedience to only four commandments isn't too bad when you realize the Jews had 613 commandments in their Scriptures.

James put the negotiated agreement in writing. The Jerusalem church sent delegates to support Paul and Barnabas, along with a written letter explaining the negotiated agreement: "Then the apostles and elders, with the whole church, decided to choose some of their own men and send them to Antioch with Paul and Barnabas. They chose Judas (called Barsabbas) and Silas, who were leaders among the believers. With them they sent the following letter" (Acts 15:22-23).

Acts 15 indicates that James explicitly modeled two of the four practices of mediation: reframing the problem and putting the solution in writing. The story in Acts is abbreviated so we don't have all the details. There is no explicit evidence in Acts indicating that James defused this volatile conflict with gentle words or supported conciliatory gestures. But in light of his letter and teaching on heavenly wisdom (James 3:13-18), it seems probable that he did use these mediation practices.

James shows us we can both fight for truth and keep the peace; we can model truth and love; we can share a gospel that demands faith in Jesus alone and live out an ethic that demonstrates love to all. James modeled what he later taught in his letter: "Peacemakers who sow in peace reap a harvest of righteousness" (James 3:18).

Think of a time when you served as a mediator. It's hard, isn't it? Mediation takes courage and comes at great cost. David W. Augsburger, currently senior professor of pastoral care and counseling at Fuller Theological Seminary, wisely notes that mediation is

- "stepping between colliding forces, competing wills, and clashing temperaments,"
- "the ability to define and clarify, to separate and discern, to link and reconcile opposites," and
- "the capacity to absorb tension, to suffer misunderstanding, to accept rejection, and to bear the pain of others' estrangement."[8]

In summary, mediators help alienated people and communities mend broken relationships.

To be effective, mediators need to be trusted. In formal mediation, a lot of attention is given to the importance of being neutral. In everyday mediation, we can't always be neutral or be perceived as neutral. But as followers of Christ, we can walk in wisdom, and when we model wisdom, people trust us. Then we have more opportunities to mediate.

Let's turn again to James for insight. He described divine wisdom as follows: "But the wisdom that comes from heaven is first of all pure; then peace-loving, considerate, submissive, full of mercy and good fruit, impartial and sincere. Peacemakers who sow in peace reap a harvest of righteousness" (James 3:17-18). He saw these character traits lived out in Jesus and calls us to model them.

Let me point out a few things about divine wisdom as it relates to mediation and repeat a few things I said earlier. First, note that James's list of traits describing wisdom begins and ends with the words *pure* and *sincere* (*sincere* literally means "without hypocrisy"). Together the two terms speak of integrity. Second, wisdom reflects beauty of character: peace-loving, considerate, full of mercy and good fruit. Third, wisdom reflects judicious thought. It is "submissive," which means it is open to reason and willing to yield. It is also "impartial" in its evaluation of people and issues. It sticks to the facts and seeks objectivity. Fourth, wisdom sows in peace, which means that mediators stay calm and speak without bludgeoning people.

Blessed are the mediators, for they are imitators of Jesus.

CONFLICT RESOLUTION

Conflict resolution is complex because there are multiple reasons for conflict. Conflict is usually caused by what the Bible calls sin—destructive patterns of behavior that rupture relationships. But there are other causes of conflict as well. In this chapter I will address one of the most frequent causes of conflict: offense. In the next, we'll look at six other causes.

I remember a particularly painful conflict I had with a coworker named Don. We were both young and zealous. We had different styles of leadership, some differences in our approach to ministry and little understanding of mediation. When I suggested that we call in our supervisor to help us sort out the issues, he replied, "We have differences, but there is no sin. I forgive you and you forgive me; so according to Matthew 18, we should not have another person involved in our dispute unless we are in sin."

What could I say?

At that time we both felt that Matthew 18 was the first and last word on peacemaking, particularly verse 15: "If a brother or sister sins, go and point out the fault, just between the two of you. If they listen to you, you have won them over." So we resolved to forgive each other and do the best we could to restore our relationship. We each wanted to be godly and believe the best of the other, but it took a long time. The pain of conflict went deep. Full restoration took years for me.

In retrospect, I believe we suffered unnecessarily. We badly needed a trusted mediator, a third party to give us perspective. We needed to realize that there is more to peacemaking than Matthew 18. Why? Because sin is not the only reason for sour relationships or conflict.

OFFENSE: A FREQUENT CAUSE OF CONFLICT

There is an important topic rarely mentioned and often neglected in books on conflict: offense. I use *offense* to describe a number of ways relationships can break down: hurt feelings, misunderstanding, different convictions, different personalities, immaturity and differences in philosophy of ministry. Offense frequently causes rifts in relationships and breaks the bond of unity. It is, therefore, a major peacemaking issue.

Offense can easily lead to sin. In fact, it usually does. But offense is not necessarily sin. For example, did Jesus ever cause offense? Did he ever hurt anyone's feelings or cause misunderstanding? Surely some scribes and Pharisees didn't appreciate Jesus calling them "hypocrites," "blind guides" and "whitewashed tombs . . . full of dead men's bones and all uncleanness" (Matthew 23 NASB)! Jesus often offended people, hurt their feelings and caused misunderstanding. But he never sinned (see 2 Corinthians 5:21; Hebrews 4:15; 1 John 3:5).

So how can we overcome these hurts, misunderstandings and differences that so often cause division? How do we deal with offense? We prepare our hearts so that we can speak the truth in love. We think through what we will say and how we will say it before we actually confront someone.

One way I prepare myself for confrontation is by simultaneously praying and envisioning what I will say to the person. (Some people prefer to write letters the offending party will never see.) Much like the psalmists shared their complaints in the presence of God (known as laments), I practice confronting the offender in the presence of God. In an imaginary conversation with the person I want to confront, I say what I feel with full emotion.

Conversations in my mind begin something like this: "Thanks for meeting with me, Bill. I was thinking about our talk the other day. You were *ugly*. I can't believe you said you would take my head off if I undermine you. That was real loving! Why are you so negative about me? Why are you so angry? What have I done to deserve this? If this is partnership, I am outta here!" In these prayerful practice rounds, I usually speak pretty harshly. You couldn't actually hear the sarcasm and angry edge in the conversation above, but it oozed from every word.

But you know what always happens when I practice? God softens my heart. The words become gentler and more precise. Then I am ready to speak the truth in love. The result would be something like this: "Thanks for meeting with me, Bill. I was thinking about our talk the other day. I am trying to understand why you would think I want to undermine you. Maybe you could share ways that I have communicated disloyalty to you in the past?" At this point I am seriously seeking to get the plank out of my eye, so I let Bill talk. Then I respond to what he said.

Then I might continue, "I also felt attacked when you said you would take my head off. Those were strong words. What have I done to cause you such consternation? Please tell me. It seemed like I pushed an emotional hot button or something." At this point I pause and silently wait for a response. Then I let him talk, and I respond.

Next I might ask, "Do you really want to partner with me? If so, I need to know how I can best work with you." I wait for Bill to respond. I conclude with one more question, "Do you often use words like 'I will take off your head'?" I listen while Bill responds.

Bill clearly had things he needed to apologize for. But I wanted to begin by focusing on my issues, asking good questions and letting him talk. Eventually he responded to my questions and conciliatory gestures by apologizing, so direct reproof was not necessary.

PEACEBUILDING COMMUNICATION

Peacemaking involves more than the eight peacemaking practices. It also demands peacebuilding communication. As noted previously, peacebuilding refers to conflict *prevention*. It focuses on cultivating loving relationships that result in a culture of peace on the team or organization.

Communication is at the heart of conflict, conflict resolution and conflict prevention. As Ken Sande says, "Words play a key role in almost every conflict. When used properly, words promote understanding and encourage agreement. When misused, they usually aggravate conflicts and drive people further apart."[9]

I had the privilege of doing mediation, peacemaking and organizational consulting for a Christian organization in the summer of 2013. We faced a seemingly intractable conflict and dysfunctional organizational practices. As was expected, this led to tense moments and periods of confusion. However, there was success on all three fronts: mediation was accomplished, peace was experienced, and organizational realignment was implemented.

We were successful for two reasons. First, the leadership team of the organization was determined to obey Jesus' teaching about peacemaking. Second, they demonstrated good communication practices. But they needed mediation because some of the leaders also had bad communication practices.

There is a spectrum of communication practices in Scripture that help build a culture of peace: accept, encourage, speak the truth in love, admonish and reprove or rebuke (see figure 6.1).

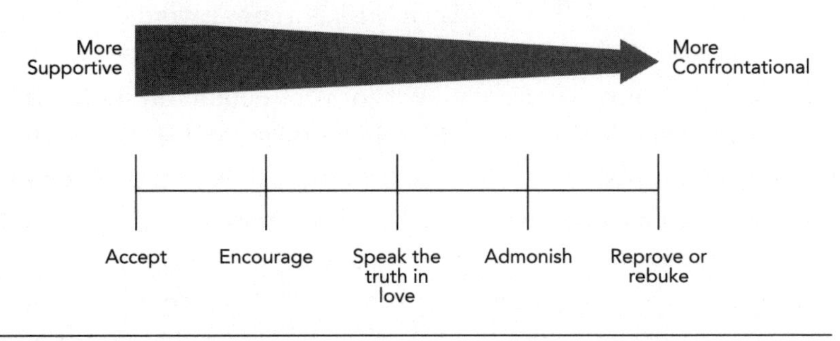

Figure 6.1

On the left side of the spectrum you find the most supportive type of communication: "Accept one another, then, just as Christ accepted you, in order to bring praise to God" (Romans 15:7). The standard for acceptance is Christ himself—the one who loved us while we were yet helpless, ungodly, sinners and even enemies (Romans 5:6-11). This reflects inclusive love and is the most affirming type of communication. We need safe, accepting relationships to be emotionally healthy and function most productively. If people feel we truly accept them, they will be more receptive to more confrontational forms of communication from us.

After acceptance is encouragement: "Therefore encourage one another and build each other up, just as in fact you are doing" (1 Thessalonians 5:11). To encourage others is to comfort them and cheer them on. It is to acknowledge specific positive actions or attributes. It is to affirm the good things we see in their lives.

Next on the continuum is the command to speak the truth *in love:* "Instead, speaking the truth in love, we will in all things grow up into him who is the head, that is, Christ" (Ephesians 4:15). Both truth and love are important. And according to this verse, truth-in-love communication is how we grow up spiritually.

Then we are called to admonish: "And concerning you, my brethren, I myself also am convinced that you yourselves are full of goodness, filled with all knowledge and able also to admonish one another" (Romans 15:14 NASB). The word *admonish* is a strong word that means to warn, advise or urge someone in a certain direction.

Finally, the most confrontational form of communication: "If a brother or sister sins against you, rebuke them, and if they repent, forgive them" (Luke 17:3). To rebuke or reprove is to express disapproval of someone's action, to warn her of the consequences of hurtful action and to try to persuade her to stop.

If we invest in people by obeying these five biblical communication practices, especially accepting, encouraging and speaking the truth in love, we are building peace. We are building equity in our relationships. Relationships are like bank accounts. You make deposits and withdrawals and check your balance. This kind of communication is a way of making "love deposits" into your relational bank account so that when potential conflict arises, your relational bank account will not be overdrawn.

This is what happened during my time mediating with the Christian organization mentioned in the story above. The reason they needed mediation in the first place was because two of the leaders' relational bank accounts had been overdrawn. Their primary communication with each other was admonishing and reproving. They did not have a foundation of accepting, encouraging and speaking the truth in love with one another, so neither listened to the other.

By contrast, the majority of the other leaders were much better at accepting, encouraging and speaking the truth in love. Because of this, when they had to admonish and rebuke, the other two leaders were receptive of their reproof.

People tend to pick and choose their preferred or natural communication type based on their personality and spiritual gifts. For example, prophetic people more naturally want to admonish and rebuke; pastors prefer encouraging and speaking the truth in love; and mercy show-ers want to accept and encourage. But all of us need to grow in all five areas.

In addition, we need to discern when to use what type of communication. The apostle Paul describes different forms of communication for different types of people. He writes, "Sisters and brothers, we urge you to

- admonish the undisciplined, irresponsible, defiant or disorderly;
- encourage the timid, fainthearted, or discouraged;
- help the weak;
- and have patience with everyone." (1 Thessalonians 5:14, my translation)

It can be counterproductive to accept or encourage people when they need to be admonished or reproved. It can reinforce their hurtful practices rather than help them grow. And it can certainly be destructive if we reprove someone who needs acceptance and encouragement.

These five types of communication are peace building in that they help prevent future conflict. They build a more peaceful future. "Peacemakers who sow in peace reap a harvest of righteousness" (James 3:18). However, they focus only on speaking. Communication is a two-way process, and it requires active listening. James gets it right again: "My dear brothers and sisters, take note of this: Everyone should be quick to listen, slow to speak and slow to become angry" (James 1:19). But the natural tendency for most of us is to be quick to speak and quick to become angry.

Being "quick to listen" means we concentrate on what the person is saying and don't just think about what we are planning to say. And good listeners don't just listen to the words. They are also sensitive to body language and the emotions behind the words. Listening is one of the most loving things we can do, because people want to be heard and understood. Good listening is crucial to both building relationships and resolving conflict. It is a profound peacebuilding skill.

The opposite is also true. Poor listening is a peace-breaking practice. During a team mediation, I encountered serious communication problems. Carlos, the team leader, was a chronic selective listener. I heard story after story of people who would share their heart and vision with Carlos only to have him ignore what they said. He would make comments or suggestions unrelated to what they shared, focusing instead on what he thought was important. The message his teammates received from him was that he did not value or appreciate them.

By contrast, Carlos's teammates were good listeners. They listened carefully to his words, read his body language and discerned the emotions behind the words. But this got them in trouble, because Carlos frequently sent mixed messages. His words said one thing, while his body language said another.

One of the big takeaways of this time together was the mantra "Good intentions are no excuse for poor communication." No one doubted Carlos's motives or integrity. His character was never in question. But the team needed a leader who communicated more effectively. So we had to have a "tough love" session with him about his chronic miscommunication. I am happy to report that Carlos was receptive to the counsel of the team and is working through these issues.

We can summarize peacebuilding communication in five points:

- Peacebuilding communication prioritizes the affirming aspects of communication so that when confrontation is necessary there is a strong relational foundation.
- Peacebuilding communication reflects/seeks congruence between words, feelings and body language.
- Peacebuilding communication means listening carefully to the words, feelings and body language of the other person and asking for clarification if necessary.
- Peacebuilding communication means you believe the best about others' motives. And if you question their motives, you ask them about it.

- Peacebuilding communication does not allow good intentions to absolve a person of bad or hurtful communication.

It may be easy for us to see how this applies in our homes and churches, but this also is relevant to national or international peacemaking. The goal of speaking and listening is to build good relationships. And relationship building is at the heart of peacemaking.

What happens in the most complex, intractable conflicts is a process of dehumanizing or demonizing "the other." The Israeli-Palestinian conflict is a good example. Through various forms of hate speech or inflammatory rhetoric, the other is vilified. It begins as categories of "us" and "them." This leads to a pattern of exclusion, with an in group and an out group. Finally it results in the confrontational mentality of us versus them.[10]

So how does one break down barriers and build bridges in conflicts like this? Through storytelling. A mediator needs to facilitate relationship building by letting people tell their stories. This builds empathy for the other and helps one begin to see things from the other's perspective.[11] According to Douglas E. Noll, storytelling increases empathy for the other and deescalates emotions. He writes, "Empirical evidence and deep experience suggest that storytelling is the only way through the conflict maze." It is "the core of a twenty-first-century approach to international negotiation."[12]

I had the privilege of experiencing this during the Building Hope Conference at the Yale Divinity School in 2011.[13] About thirty Muslim, Christian and Jewish leaders came from Jordan, Israel, Turkey, Indonesia, the Philippines, the United Arab Emirates and the United States. These women and men leaders, chosen because of their record of leadership and potential, attended this international gathering focused on seeking the common good.

The ten-day conference was structured to build relationships between the participants. We started with the easier topics and progressed to the more controversial as the days went on. We had meals together, breaks for informal discussion and two excursions to get to know each other more personally. And we did one thing at this conference that I had never done before: let everyone share their personal stories.

The stories about life in Israel and Palestine were the most poignant. Rabbi Abraham from Israel shared how he lived in fear, haunted by the memory of his grandmother being killed on a bus by a suicide bomber. This personal story melted the hearts of Muslims who traditionally view Israelis only as evil oppressors. Stories of teenage Israeli soldiers degrading and intimidating both Muslims and Christians in the Holy Land softened the hearts of Jewish leaders, helping them view their protagonists in a more sympathetic, positive light. When we finally talked about the Israeli-Palestinian conflict, there wasn't a dry eye in the room.

Storytelling personalizes the other and helps build bridges.

7

HOW PEACE CATALYSTS WORK ON TEAMS AND IN ORGANIZATIONS

The conversation isn't about the relationship. The conversation is the relationship. We effect change by engaging in robust conversations with others and ourselves.

SUSAN SCOTT

For more than forty years, I have been a student of teams and organizations. I have served as a pastor, led numerous crosscultural teams and birthed and directed a global network that grew to eighty organizations. I have worked as a CEO in a large, international nonprofit organization that serves in over seventy countries, and most recently I started Peace Catalyst International.

In all this I've learned that there's a profound relationship between peacemaking and productivity. You don't need to be a rocket scientist to realize that good relationships increase output. Harmony enhances productivity. The inverse is also true. *Broken relationships hinder productivity.* We may have grand visions and lofty dreams. We can talk all we want about changing the world. But if we don't handle conflict well, our impact will be diminished.

Dan Dana, the founder of Mediation Training Institute International, has demonstrated conclusively that conflict results in financial loss. Dana has developed a calculator that estimates this principle. Hours wasted or efficiency hindered equals money lost.[1]

Understanding team dynamics and cultivating conflict resolution competencies give us tools to facilitate harmony and maximize impact (if you work in a nonprofit organization) or to facilitate peace and maximize profit (if you work in the business world). If we apply these practices to the workplace, we save time, we save money and we save relationships.

FOUR STAGES OF TEAM LIFE: FORMING, STORMING, NORMING AND PERFORMING[2]

Startup organizations and new teams usually go through these four stages before they are productive. *Forming* refers to the beginning stage of team life. The team is fired up and ready to change the world. Expectations are unclear. Members test the water. And interactions are superficial. This is the honeymoon stage.

Storming is the inevitable conflict between team members as well as their resistance to the group's tasks and structure. This is the time when the team members struggle through their differences. There are healthy and unhealthy types of storming. You know you are storming in healthy ways when the team either stays together, despite changes, or team members choose to leave with the blessing and well wishes of the team. The goal is to work through healthy types of storming and minimize unhealthy types. Unfortunately, since we live in a broken, wounded world, unhealthy storming will take place.

Norming is group cohesion. Members accept the team and develop norms for resolving conflicts, making decisions and completing assignments. Norming takes place in at least three ways. As team members grow through the storming stage, they become more relaxed and steady. Conflicts no longer throw the team off course. Norming also takes place when the team develops some kind of routine. Scheduled team meetings of various kinds give a sense of predictability and orientation.

Norming is cultivated through team-building events and activities. Celebrations, public and private affirmation, retreats and fun get-togethers are practical ways to help a team norm and move toward the performing stage. Norming is a necessary transition and is, in fact, an essential part of performing. A team can't move to performing without norming.

Performing is the payoff stage. At this point the team has weathered relational storming. It has developed its relationships, structure and purpose. It bears fruit and enjoys productivity.

Yet, in a sense, these dynamics are cyclical. Teams go through ever-deepening levels of storming, norming and performing. Furthermore, one individual on the team may be storming with one teammate and performing with another. Thus these stages merely give a rough outline of the growth dynamics of any team or organization. (From now on, I will use the words *team* and *organization* interchangeably.)

Experience has shown that understanding these four stages will help you anticipate and be prepared for problems ahead. A grasp of these stages will keep you from unnecessary pain and make you more effective. They provide a helpful road map for teams. Leaders know what to expect and so do team members. Review these stages with your team, using them to discuss how you can be more fruitful in fulfilling your organizational purposes.

SIX STEPPING STONES TO PERFORMING

It is one thing to know that teams go through a storming phase. It is quite another to know how to handle this stage in constructive ways. And you can't get to performing without storming. Let's face it, conflict can sabotage productivity. And it's painful!

I have found that conflict crops up in six major areas. I refer to these as the six stumbling blocks of storming—or, better said, the six stepping stones to performing:

- character problems
- growing pains
- cultural differences
- gifting fit
- vision or values differences
- personality differences

Just knowing there are six chronic areas of conflict on teams is important. But it is even more important to learn how to turn stumbling blocks of storming into stepping stones to performing. We can learn how to do this from three biblical stories. They don't teach us all we need to know on the subject, but they illustrate the issues, providing a window into the nature of these six recurring conflict zones.

CONFLICT ON JESUS' TEAM

Character Problems

Every experienced leader knows that character problems cause conflict and hinder team productivity. Even Jesus faced character problems on his team (Mark 10:35-45). Two of his two disciples, James and John, jockeyed for seats of power and prestige. They coveted the special place of honor next to Jesus. The result? The rest of the team was upset by their power play. They were angry over James and John's blatant display of pride. It's not clear why they were indignant, but maybe it was because they wanted the top seats themselves.

We can turn the stumbling block of character problems like these into a stepping stone of growth through the peacemaking practices outlined in this book. We return again to the five essential practices of conflict resolution:

- Take responsibility.
- Lovingly reprove.
- Accept reproof.
- Ask for forgiveness.
- Forgive others.

The application of these five practices as well as the peacebuilding communication practices of Scripture helps us deal with and overcome character problems.

Imagine what might have happened in this conflict between James, John and the rest of the apostles if they had applied Jesus' teaching on conflict resolution. Let's assume Jesus wasn't present, so they had to deal with each other as a team.

Here's one possible scenario: James and John get angry because the team is mad at them. (Typical so far.) But as they start to raise their voices in anger, John feels a check in his spirit: "Don't get angry at the team's response. You need to take responsibility for your part in this quarrel." So John takes James aside for a moment to share what he senses God is saying to him.

Then they quietly ask the Lord to show them the log in their own eyes (see Matthew 7:3-5). The Lord whispers, "Your personal ambition is wrong. Seeking to outmaneuver your teammates for top positions is not right. I have called you to humble, sacrificial service, not self-exalting positions of power." The light goes on. So James and John confess their selfishness to the team and ask for forgiveness.

But, as you might expect, the others doubt their sincerity. "You can't get away with this kind of proud, self-promotion so easily," they say. "We are apostles too!"

The Lord, however, says to Peter, "Remember what Jesus said to you when you asked him how often you should forgive the person who sins against you?"

"Seventy times seven times," Peter responds. Then he says to the others, "Okay, guys, we need to forgive James and John." So the apostles accept their apology.

Conflict resolved. Unity restored. The five essential practices of conflict resolution help us turn the stumbling block of character problems into stepping stones of growth. They also help us address the remaining five stumbling blocks.

CONFLICT IN THE EARLY CHURCH

Growing Pains, Cultural Diversity and Gifting Fit

Fast-forward to Jesus' team a few years later. Acts 6:1-6 describes a fascinating account of conflict resolution in the early church. This story centers on a specific church problem, but it also describes three kinds of challenges that most leaders face today: increased cultural diversity, rapid growth and outdated (or irrelevant) organizational structures. Here's what happened:

> But as the believers rapidly multiplied, there were rumblings of discontent. The Greek-speaking believers complained about the Hebrew-speaking believers, saying that their widows were being discriminated against in the daily distribution of food. So the Twelve called a meeting of all the believers. They said, "We apostles should spend our time teaching the word of God, not running a food program. . . . Select seven men who are well respected and are full of the Spirit and wisdom. We will give them this responsibility. Then we apostles can spend our time in prayer and teaching the word." Everyone liked this idea, and they chose the following: Stephen (a man full of faith and the Holy Spirit), Philip, Procorus, Nicanor, Timon, Parmenas, and Nicolas of Antioch (an earlier convert to the Jewish faith). These seven were presented to the apostles, who prayed for them as they laid their hands on them. (Acts 6:1-6 NLT)

What happens when organizational growth strains your structures and stretches your leaders beyond their capacity? Did you notice how

Luke described this conflict? "There were rumblings of discontent."

Growth pains alone have caused their fair share of conflict in organizations, just as they did in early church. This kind of conflict emerges primarily from change rather than character problems per se. When organizations grow numerically, their capacity gets strained. Old structures and leadership abilities for one stage of growth often do not work well for a larger organization. They need to adjust to this new reality.

Organizational growth usually demands reevaluation of structures and people's strengths and competencies. Leaders need to determine if their current structure meets the needs of their growing organization and to change accordingly. They also need to evaluate whether or not their leaders have the capacity to grow with the organization. Sometimes they do; sometimes they don't. If they don't have the capacity, they need to be redeployed and a new leader appointed. These kinds of changes aren't easy.

It is also worth noting that external change, whether in the marketplace, the environment or other arenas, can lead to potential organizational conflict as well. The most obvious example is the impact of terrorism, globalization and pluralism in the twenty-first century. These paradigm shifts demand change at many levels.[3]

Adjusting to change demands deep conversations that often lead to misunderstanding and sometimes conflict. So knowing and practicing the five essential practices of conflict resolution, along with peacebuilding communication, gives leaders and organizations important skills necessary to navigate change.

How do you handle cultural diversity in your organization? Cultural diversity is a major source of conflict on teams and in organizations. It was even an issue in the early church. Apparently, those who were distributing food were taking care of the Hebrew-speaking widows and ignoring the Greek-speaking widows. It is unclear whether this conflict was actually due to prejudice or just to poor administration because of growth pains. But whatever the reason, the church was becoming multicultural while the leadership team remained monocultural (Hebrew-speaking Jews only). So how did they handle it?

It seems that the apostles remembered what Jesus taught them about servant leadership (Mark 10:35-45). So rather than dictating what the team needed to do, they modeled participatory leadership. They shared their decision-making power with the church.

The apostles set forth guidelines to choose new leadership, but they also involved the church in the choosing of new leaders: "Brothers and sisters, choose seven men from among you who are known to be full of the Spirit and wisdom. We will turn this responsibility over to them" (Acts 6:3). This wasn't pure democracy, but it wasn't top-down leadership either. Rather, the apostles facilitated an interactive process of decision making.

The result? All seven of the leaders chosen had Greek names. The very people most hurt in this conflict were chosen to lead the group out of conflict. In this case, conflict was productive. By giving guidelines and allowing the participation of the cultural minority, the apostles wisely led the early church through the conflict into becoming a multicultural community.

Conflicts over cultural differences will only increase on our teams and organizations because we live in an increasingly interconnected, mobile, multicultural world. Living in a multicultural world demands cultural intelligence. A high IQ isn't enough. We need a high CQ (cultural quotient). So let me make a few important observations about culture that should help increase your CQ.

The Bible affirms cultural *diversity.* The New Testament describes how the gospel spread from a Jewish culture to a multicultural world. In this transition, God did not force Gentile churches to live up to Jewish cultural expectations (Acts 15). The Bible does not assume the superiority of one culture over another. In fact, ethnic diversity will remain throughout eternity, as people from every tongue, tribe and nation worship the Lord in endless, exuberant praise (Revelation 7:9-12).

The Bible encourages not only cultural diversity but also cultural *duality.* Every culture is rich in beauty and goodness while at the same time tainted by sin and evil. Every culture contains a mixture of virtue and vice, good and evil.

So all cultures must be tested and evaluated by Scripture. Cultural diversity and cultural duality demand cultural *discernment.* And effective cultural discernment requires wisdom and humility. Why? Because our natural tendency is to see the demonic in other cultures or the neutral-but-different aspects of culture in a negative light. We need to get the plank out of our own cultural eye before we get the speck out of the other's cultural eye. What Jesus taught about personal reconciliation relates to clashes over cultural differences as well. In addition, people with a high CQ focus on the positive elements in the culture of the other (especially in the early stages of learning).

Paul's counsel applies here: "Brothers and sisters, whatever is true, whatever is noble, whatever is right, whatever is pure, whatever is lovely, whatever is admirable—if anything is excellent or praiseworthy—think about such things" (Philippians 4:8). Just as personalities have strengths and weaknesses, so do cultures. For example, the Sundanese of Indonesia are a hospitable, gentle and patient people, excelling in virtues that most Americans lack. However, they struggle deeply over forgiveness and honesty. Asking for forgiveness is to submit to the power of the person from whom they are seeking forgiveness, so the supplicant is left weak and vulnerable. And honesty exposes them to possible exploitation by others. The one confessing could later have the confession used against him. We saw this happen on many occasions; their fears were real.

Nevertheless, the Bible exhorts us to uphold cultural values that are right and to correct values that are wrong. We had to tell our Sundanese friends that even though their culture viewed asking for forgiveness and honest confession as undesirable, this is what Jesus was asking them to do. And not only that, his blessing was on them: "Blessed are the poor in spirit. . . . Blessed are the meek. . . . Blessed are those who are persecuted because of righteousness" (Matthew 5:3, 5, 10).

Some cultural traits are neither right nor wrong, just different. Let me illustrate from my experience in Indonesia. Americans tend to be time oriented; Indonesians tend to be event oriented. This means that Americans live by the clock, while Indonesians focus more on what is happening in the here and now. Americans place a greater value on productivity, while Indonesians stress relationship. Americans stop a conversation if they have another appointment, while Indonesians tend to keep talking. To adjust, I threw away my planner for the first few years I lived in Indonesia.

Americans tend to be direct in communication while Indonesians tend to be indirect. For example, when someone comes to us in America, we quickly ask something like, "How can I help you?" or "What's up?" But this direct approach to communication often offends Indonesians, who value being less straightforward. I remember how hard it was for me to adjust to the Indonesian value of drinking tea and chitchatting for forty-five minutes before bringing up what I really wanted to talk about.

Anyone working on a multicultural team must seek to understand and appreciate the differing values of teammates. Following apostolic practice and modeling participatory leadership is one way to begin the process. We learn by listening and problem solving together. There are also many resources available to help us grow in cultural intelligence and increase our CQ.[4]

The problem the church faced was not just rapid growth or multiculturalism. They also had an organizational (or leadership) structure that no longer met the needs of the church. The apostles needed to remain focused on the task God gave them, which was to pray and minister the Word. They needed to be good stewards of their gifts. But they also needed to serve the whole congregation. So they had to delegate the ministry of serving the widows to those within the church who were motivated and gifted to do so. One of the biggest challenges leaders face is to match the right people with the right jobs.

The apostles handled this relational storming by making structural change. They added another level of leadership to handle the numerical growth. They wisely addressed gifting alignment that facilitated the next stage of organizational growth.

PAUL VS. BARNABAS
Values and Personality Differences

Leaders disagree, sparks fly, and teams divide. Been there. Done that. But take heart. Even great leaders clash. Two of my favorite leaders in the Bible—Paul and Barnabas—had a "sharp disagreement" that led to a team split. What caused this split, and what can we learn from it?

> After some days Paul said to Barnabas, "Let us return and visit the brethren in every city in which we proclaimed the word of the Lord, and see how they are." Barnabas wanted to take John, called Mark, along with them also. But Paul kept insisting that they should not take him along who had deserted them in Pamphylia and had not gone with them to the work. And there occurred such a sharp disagreement that they separated from one another, and Barnabas took Mark with him and sailed away to Cyprus. But Paul chose Silas and left, being committed by the brethren to the grace of the Lord. (Acts 15:36-40 NASB)

What went wrong? Paul and Barnabas had a clash of personalities and values. They knew *what* they wanted to accomplish (the vision). But their conflict revolved around *how* they did things (the values).

Paul was task oriented, while Barnabas was relationally oriented. Paul had a type-A personality—ambitious, demanding and hard driving—while Barnabas was more pastoral, a mentor who loved to develop people. Mark left the team on their first journey, so according to Paul, he did not deserve a second chance. By contrast, Barnabas, known as "the son of encouragement" (Acts 4:36), felt Mark deserved another opportunity.

This conflict was not an issue of sin. They were storming over differing approaches to people and differing values. Both men had their strengths. I fully understand their different orientations to ministry. I have seen too many conflicts like this, and frankly I have realized that I am not called to side with only one personality type or philosophy of ministry. God loves diversity and uses different styles of leadership. So here are three lessons gleaned from this kind of conflict that can help us from being ambushed.

1. Paul and Barnabas needed a mediator to help them work out their differences. A mediator, or go-between, may not have persuaded Paul and Barnabas to change their perspectives. But a mediator may have helped them discern a better way forward than splitting up. At the very least, this intervention could have helped them minimize the pain of separation. Let's try to imagine Paul and Barnabas's "sharp disagreement" and how a mediator might have helped them.

Paul: Mark is a failure! He deserted us during our first journey, so the odds are he'll do it again. Mark can't be trusted. We've got important work to do and can't waste time with weak people like him.

Barnabas: Remember, Paul, I stood with you when no one believed in you. Because of me, the church leaders in Jerusalem accepted you. I supported you when no one else did. I believe Mark needs my support now as well.

Paul: Mark might need your support, but I am more concerned about reaching the Gentiles. That is my calling. You are putting family above fruitfulness. Your concern to support your cousin is more important to you than fruitful ministry among those who have never heard of Christ.

Barnabas: Let me remind you of your past. You were a terrorist. You are still an angry man. Remember that I mentored you in the early days, even though you once tried to destroy the church. I want to mentor Mark in the same way.

Paul: Barnabas, you've lost your vision for those without Christ. I don't want to get distracted from our main calling by having to worry about taking care of Mark. This is not personal, Barnabas. It's a matter of principle.

Barnabas: No, Paul, I have not lost my vision. I want to raise up the next generation of workers. So I am willing to work with people who have experienced failure.

Mediator to Paul and Barnabas: Men, please, you both have strong convictions about these issues, but your emotions are getting the best of you. Both of you are exaggerating to make your point. You have begun attacking each other rather than the problem. Let's be more accurate with our words, okay? Can we try to find a win-win solution?

Mediator to Paul: I would like to make a few observations. One failure does not mean that Mark *is* a failure. You can't generalize from one incident by insisting that because Mark deserted you, he is therefore a failure. You have interpreted the fact of his desertion in the worst possible light, Paul. You should look at this with different lenses. Don't forget that Jesus gave people a second chance. Remember how Jesus lovingly restored Peter after he denied him three times. Are you really such an either-or thinker, Paul? Isn't it possible to choose both family and ministry?

Mediator to Barnabas: I am sure you can appreciate Paul's concern. No one likes to invest time and energy in someone who lets them down when the going gets tough. Have you helped Mark grow through this situation? Do you really think he is ready to persevere on this trip? Can you empathize with Paul's idea for what this trip is all about? Paul's primary goal is to share the gospel and make disciples. He wants to plant churches. He does not see this as a training mission.

Mediator to Paul and Barnabas: My goal is to help you two discern what the problem is that is causing the conflict and come up with a mutually agreed-upon solution. My role is to help the process, while it is your responsibility to make a deal that is fair to both of you. So let's look at the situation with a new lens. Let's reframe it and see if we can come up with a win-win situation. . . .

The mediator may have helped them stay together and take Mark with them. We can only guess what might have been. But note: the wise leader proactively finds a mediator before conflict escalates. And the wise organization proactively prepares for conflict. Organizations can train some of their own people to serve as mediators, thus preventing potentially destructive conflicts.

At the same time we need to acknowledge that there are times godly men and women, with different personalities and values, need to agree to disagree. Rather than striving to maintain one team, it is sometimes wise to divide it into two. Though important, mediation can't solve everything.

A significant postscript to this conflict: eventually Paul was reconciled to Mark and valued his ministry: "Get Mark and bring him with you, because he is helpful to me in my ministry" (2 Timothy 4:11; see also Colossians 4:10; Philemon 24). I wonder if Barnabas played a role in mediating between them.

2. ***Paul and Barnabas needed to write a memo of understanding (MOU).*** Like Paul and Barnabas, many teams get ambushed by conflict because certain aspects of their vision and values have not been explicitly stated. Most teams do fairly well regarding the vision. But if values, priorities and practices are not explicit, disputes often arise.

An MOU is a covenant-like document that outlines the vision, values, priorities and practices of the team.[5] The writing of an MOU encourages the leader to clarify the team's ethos or allows the team to participate in the process of articulating its approach (depending on how the team works). Either way, this helps the team understand expectations. To facilitate unity of purpose on teams, all the team members sign the MOU—indicating their commitment to the team's vision and values.

I have found the MOU to be a valuable tool for teams—something I have used for over twenty-five years. But for the MOU to play a unifying role on the team, the leader needs to model and communicate the vision and values *repeatedly.*[6] What is written in the MOU also needs to be a reviewed on an ongoing basis.

An MOU will not end conflict. It will merely help minimize conflict over differences in philosophy of ministry. Here is a sample MOU:

Memo of Understanding

Name of organization or team:

Purpose:

The purpose of this Memo of Understanding (MOU) is to clarify expectations on the team. It describes the vision, values, and strategy of ______________. Team members must be in agreement with this MOU, or have the consent of the team leader regarding any disagreement.

Vision:
Mission:
Values:
Strategy (plans and policy):
Decision making:
Conflict resolution:

I/we have carefully read and agree with the team MOU (Memorandum of Understanding). Upon signing this, I/we agree to abide and uphold the team MOU.

____

Signature Date

____

Signature Date

3. Paul and Barnabas needed to understand and appreciate personality differences. God has created us each with particular gifts and temperaments. We each have different styles of leading and unique personalities. Biblical authors reflect this same kind of diversity. Paul wrote differently than Peter, James or John. Their styles were determined partly by the problems they addressed and partly by their personalities.

Personality differences can lead to conflict or to productivity—depending on how the differences are handled. Every organization needs a healthy mix of different personalities. We need visionaries to point us in the right direction, detail people in the area of logistics and accounting, and encouragers to keep us all together.

Every personality has its unique strengths and weaknesses, yet just like culture, every personality must be evaluated in light of Scripture. The Word of God cuts across every type of personality, affirming strengths and correcting weaknesses.

Introverts are called to sacrificial love, even if they don't like to reach out beyond themselves. Extroverts are called to humility, even if they are tempted to parade around like peacocks. I'll never forget one day when my wife and I were counseling another couple. The woman vehemently objected to the counsel we were giving her because it wasn't natural for her personality type. We reminded her that our personality type never excuses us from obedience to Scripture.

More recently I was doing some marriage counseling with a young, extroverted leader. He was the major cause of conflict in his marriage, so I exhorted him from 1 Peter 3:7 about the need to live with his more introverted wife in an understanding way. He blurted out, "But I am extremely extroverted. I need to have people constantly around me."

I said, "The apostle Peter expects you to live with your wife in an understanding way. He didn't include an exclusion clause for extroverts."

Frustration and misunderstanding between different personalities result in needless conflicts. So to maintain healthy team life, we must acknowledge and appreciate personality differences. Learn about the strengths and weaknesses of each personality type and how different personalities can best work together. Having a firm grasp of personality differences helps us minimize conflict and maximize impact.[7]

RECOURSE FOR RESOLVING CONFLICT

Understanding the practice of recourse is one way to minimize destructive conflict and maximize impact. Recourse is not explicitly taught in Scripture, but the concept fits with the principles of peacemaking. With recourse, we appeal to someone higher up in the organization if we strongly disagree with the one at the level of authority just above us, whom I'll call a supervisor. This does not mean that we go around the supervisor to make our appeal. Rather, recourse means that we go *through* the supervisor to appeal to his or her supervisor (see figure 7.1).

In other words, if several attempts at seeking to speak the truth in love to the supervisor have failed, we then tell the supervisor that we are going to appeal to the person over him. We also tell him exactly what we are going to say. If we need to resort to recourse in decentralized international organizations, it may mean we begin the process via email. If this is the case, we write our appeal to the higher authority but then copy our supervisor as well.

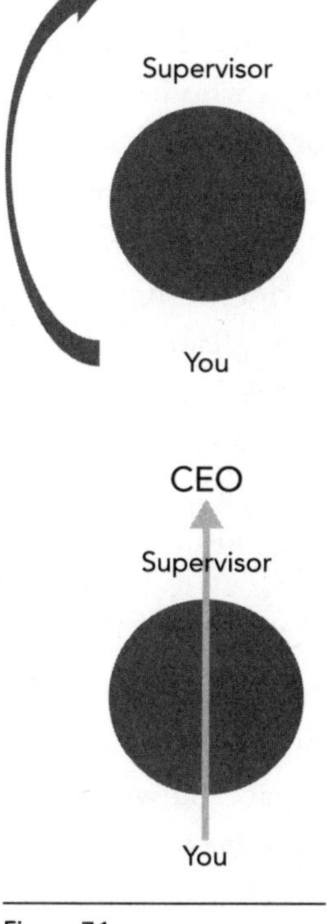

Figure 7.1

Recourse honors four peacemaking principles:

- It prevents gossip.
- It honors our leaders.
- It encourages truthful communication.
- The person taking recourse honors Jesus by taking the initiative in peacemaking.

When I first joined Frontiers, an interdenominational mission agency, in 1984, I noticed that it attracted a lot of entrepreneurial activists, just like me. We had strong personalities and most of us were in a rush to get things done. We were the "bad boys" of mission, going where no one had gone before (or so we thought), daring to do it differently (and we thought *better*) from what others had done. We were bold, all right. But our arrogance annoyed other mission agency personnel, embarrassed our wives and frustrated our teammates.

It wasn't long before a team member, whose team was doing good work in a particularly harsh and hostile environment, shattered our glittering image of ourselves. She tried on multiple occasions to appeal to her team leader regarding policies and procedures, but to no avail. Frustrated, she finally contacted the international office. She asked them who in the organization was holding team leaders accountable for their work and behavior. She wanted to know where in the organization was a plan for recourse should a problem between a team member and team leader become intractable.

Her strong appeal prevented future team blowups. And she was right. Team leaders weren't always wise, and they certainly weren't always good at listening to teammates. Frontiers saved a lot of us by implementing a policy of recourse. If a team member believed he was not being heard by his team leader, he now had a way to make his voice heard.

CONSTRUCTIVE AND DESTRUCTIVE CONFLICT

Every team and organization wants to minimize conflict and maximize impact. But not all conflict is bad. In fact, healthy conflict maximizes impact. So what makes conflict constructive and what makes it destructive? How do we cultivate healthy conflict and diminish destructive conflict?

Constructive conflict involves wrestling deeply with ideas, issues and decisions that must be made. We speak the truth in love in order to persuade others about our convictions. Disagreement and vigorous debate help teams discern better ways of doing things. This kind of conflict helps organizations find the best possible solutions to their problems. We need to encourage robust conflict that centers on different ideas and opinions.

Destructive conflict, by contrast, takes place when someone begins to attack another person instead of attacking the problem. The aggressor might verbally pummel the person instead of seeking a solution. Mean-spirited comments or sarcastic remarks aimed at putting a person down or winning an argument damage team morale and hinder productivity.

Patrick Lencioni describes a continuum of different conflict dynamics (see figure 7.2).[8] On one end of the spectrum is artificial harmony. At the other end is personal attack. The ideal is somewhere near the middle.

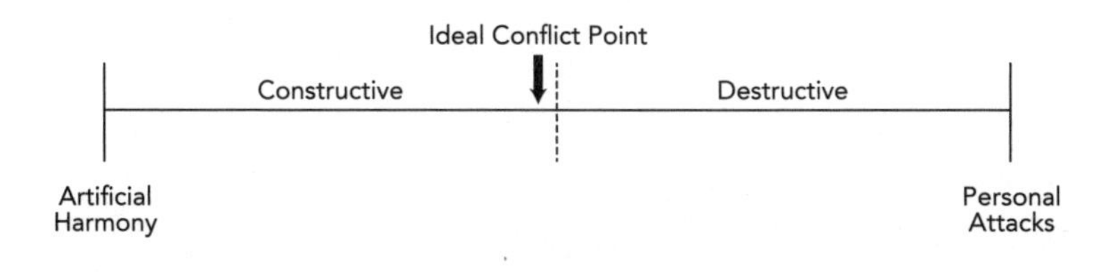

Figure 7.2

When I was international director of Frontiers, I would convene working groups to wrestle with important issues in our organization. We addressed issues like the role of women in leadership, the impact of globalization on the mission of the church and the crafting of a new mission statement. All of these topics were controversial or at least potentially controversial.

Because of this, we chose some of the best men and women in the organization to deliberate and debate the issues—to discern *what* to do and *how* to do it. We always began our meetings by inviting everyone to come up with guidelines for positive dialogue. We established agreed-upon ground rules as the basis for our interaction. Here are examples of guidelines that usually made the list:

- We will speak the truth in love.
- We will preserve confidentiality.
- We will check our hats at the door. We will put aside our organizational titles and roles because in this meeting we are equals.

- We will work toward consensus.
- We will attack problems, not people.
- Those who aren't arguing for a position will act as peacemakers.
- If you are silent on an issue, it means you are in agreement.

Constructive conflict was part of the program. We were fond of describing meetings like these as "iron sharpening iron" times, based on Proverbs 27:17: "As iron sharpens iron, so one person sharpens another."

8

HOW PEACE CATALYSTS SPREAD THE PEACE

PART ONE: SOCIAL PEACEMAKING

The church is a peace institute . . . a group of people who . . . embody peace in anticipation of that day when God establishes peace in all his creation. . . . Numerous schools for war exist. . . . Few people study peace. The church should be a place where people study and practice peace.

KLYNE SNODGRASS

SOCIAL PEACEMAKING

My friend Jeff Burns is one of the leaders of Peace Catalyst International. He is passionate about promoting peace and reconciliation between Muslims and Christians. But he has not always felt that way. I'll let him tell his story in his own words.

> Prior to 2005, I hated Muslims. I would not have admitted that openly, but my deepest feelings toward them were resentment, distrust and bitterness. I was a conservative Christian minister, and I taught parishioners that it was appropriate to love Jews and

to support the nation of Israel unconditionally. I also taught that the descendants of Ishmael, especially Arabs, were a mistake that Abraham made with his servant girl Hagar. My attitude changed dramatically one afternoon in a Starbucks, when I had an encounter with a Muslim boy named Omar.

Three months before I met Omar, I had been invited to attend a class at a church in the area on Muslim/Christian relationships. I laughed at the invitation when I received it. My wife, Sheila, told me she felt I should attend the class because I had a deep prejudice against Muslims, especially Arabs. I had always prided myself on being a progressive pastor who promoted racial reconciliation in the churches that I had led, but when it came to Muslims, I held on to my prejudice.

I told Sheila that the only way I would attend this class was if Jesus himself appeared at the foot of my bed and told me to. I said, "Then I would ask for his identification to make sure it was really him." After some prodding, however, and prayer on the part of my wife, I finally decided to take the class.

As I read books on Islam and attended the class, I began to realize that I was judging and condemning a group of people that I knew little about. I read Muslim, Christian and secular authors on Islam. I made a point to hear all sides. Although the class and the books I was reading were impacting my view of Muslims, my heart was not ready for a complete turnaround.

One day I was sitting in a Starbucks, reading a book about Muslims and their culture. The more I read the book, the more frustrated I became. I felt like I was reading about aliens from another planet. I decided to pray for guidance on this issue. I closed the book I was reading and prayed silently that God would show me what to do. I prayed, "God, surely you are not calling me to reach out to Muslims in friendship and to build bridges between Christians and Muslims. I want you to know that I have no desire to do this, because it would stretch me way beyond my comfort zone. But if you are calling me, I need you to give me a sign so clear I will never doubt it."

I went back to drinking my coffee, feeling a sense of relief because I did not believe he would answer that prayer. Within a couple of minutes, however, a little boy walked over to my table and asked if he could borrow one of the highlighters that I was using to mark my book. I said, "Sure, you can borrow the blue one."

He said, "I prefer the orange one." He took the orange highlighter, got in a chair next to me and said, "By the way, my name is Omar. I am five years old, and I am here to teach you Arabic." On his shirt was the logo of the local Islamic elementary school.

I was stunned. I could imagine God laughing and saying, "You didn't think that I could answer that prayer, did you?" Omar's mother called to him to leave me alone. I told her that Omar was fine, that I did not mind him hanging out with me. God had my complete attention.

Omar began writing the Arabic alphabet and coaching me on how to do it. He told me that I was doing it all wrong, and then he attempted to guide my hand. This went on for about thirty minutes. Afterward I approached his mother and told her that I believed Omar would be a great teacher one day. She told me that he was a shy child, and he did not typically approach strangers. So she wondered what had compelled him to come over to me. Although I thought I knew the answer, I did not tell her. As I left Starbucks that day, I began my journey of walking with Muslims as friends.

SOCIAL PEACEMAKING AND MEDIATION

During a Vineyard Great Lakes Regional Conference in Columbus, Ohio, in May 2012, Yale theologian and peacemaker Miroslav Volf shared with the pastors in attendance a story about the Common Word Dialogue[1] between Christians and Muslims at Yale: "Prior to the dialogue, we inserted a brief apology in the Yale response to the Common Word, asking Muslims for forgiveness. People got so upset! They said you should not ask for forgiveness until Muslims ask for forgiveness first!" Volf paused, and with a big smile on his face asked, "Since when is my moral behavior predicated on the moral behavior of another?"

In his book *Christians Are Hate-Filled Hypocrites . . . and Other Lies You've Been Told,* Bradley R. E. Wright notes that Christians do very well ethically as compared to the rest of society. We are neighborly, forgiving and caring for the poor. He also demonstrates that general good will toward others increases with church attendance.

However, Wright also admits that Christians in general and evangelicals in particular do not like people of different races, religion and sexual orientation.[2] Evangelicals seem to struggle most with three communities: Muslims, undocumented immigrants (usually Latinos) and the LGBT community.

Yet the commands to pursue peace with everyone, to love our neighbor and to love our enemy push us toward these very communities (or whatever other community you or your church struggles with). This is the outward or social dimension of peacemaking. And it is different from interpersonal peacemaking. The most important difference is this: interpersonal peacemaking focuses on conflict between individuals, whereas social peacemaking addresses conflict between groups. Some of the most prominent group conflicts include gender conflict (males versus females), class conflict (rich versus poor), religious conflict (Christians versus Muslims), racial conflict (black versus white) and conflicts over sexual orientation (evangelicals versus the gay community).

This group-versus-group focus compounds the complexity of peacemaking. But there are also simple steps we can take in social peacemaking. That's why I like to talk about the "simplexity" of peacemaking in seminars.[3] Peacemaking is both simple and complex at the same time.

Social peacemaking can be truly simple, however, when the individual peacemaker reaches out to the other in a Christlike manner. Fran was talking to an African American man who worked at an airport as a companion for disabled passengers. He shared how different African Americans are from Africans. He used the Somalis as an example. He said, "Somali women get very nervous if I touch them or sit close to them. So I have had to learn about their culture and have tried to respect them by not treating them like I would an African American woman. This simple act of respecting their culture makes a big difference."

A woman attended a Love Your Neighbor Dinner, where Christians and Muslims gather to discuss love of neighbor and enjoy a meal together.[4] That simple experience of meeting Muslims in a setting of love helped her see that they are people just like her. She said, "I no longer fear Muslims. In the past when I saw a woman wearing a head covering [*hijab*] at a store, I was fearful and avoided her. Now I go up to her and greet her warmly." So social peacemaking isn't always complicated.

Why is there conflict between groups? Group conflict often arises out of cultural, racial or religious differences that then lead to prejudice, fear, hatred, ignorance and misunderstanding. The result is often deadly.

The group conflict between the Jews and Samaritans of Jesus' time has profound parallels with the modern conflict between Christians and Muslims: both include racial and religious tensions. Jews and Samaritans were monotheists. Jews and Samaritans worshiped the God of Abraham. Yet the Samaritans were seen as heretics—syncretistic in faith, ethnically inferior, excluded from the true worship of God.

The animosity and hostility between these two communities is explicitly mentioned twice in the Gospels:

> Therefore the Samaritan woman said to Him, "How is it that You, being a Jew, ask me for a drink since I am a Samaritan woman?" (For Jews have no dealings with Samaritans). (John 4:9 NASB)

> But the people there [Samaritans] did not welcome him [Jesus], because he was heading for Jerusalem. When the disciples James

> and John saw this, they asked, "Lord, do you want us to call fire down from heaven to destroy them?" But Jesus turned and rebuked them. (Luke 9:53-55)

The similarities are stunning. James's and John's hostile response to the Samaritans did not reflect the Spirit of Jesus. Yet it is hauntingly similar to how some Christians respond to Muslims today.

Jesus' personal interaction with the Samaritan woman in John 4 provides divine guidance on addressing the other, whether the other is a Muslim or any other group despised, feared or hated by Christians. Jesus began by purposely putting himself among Samaritans. He actually engineered the encounter by taking the initiative to engage the Samaritan woman. Instead of expressing the animosity or hostility typical of Jewish-Samaritan interaction, he began a discussion that would build a bridge with the Samaritan.

Jesus didn't engage in nice interfaith dialogue. Nor did he want to argue about religion. He began with dialogue *and* addressed doctrine, clearly stating that salvation was from the Jews (John 4:22). But he didn't say she had to *be* a Jew to be saved. Instead he talked about the new thing God was doing ("his worshipers must worship in the Spirit and in truth," John 4:24). And he told her that he was the coming Messiah. In other words, faith was not about the temple or a holy mountain or outward forms of worship. Those who worshiped (heretically) what they did not know were now able to become true worshipers if they worshiped in spirit and truth—without becoming Jews. This true faith and new thing centered on Jesus as the Messiah.

Jesus overcame religious, racial, gender, educational and even moral barriers to connect with the Samaritan woman. No condemnation. No finger wagging. No debate. Bridges of love. Bridges that led her to himself. That was Jesus one-on-one with the Muslims of his day.

The first step in social peacemaking is proactively engaging the other. Paul made this clear in Romans 12:18: "If it is possible, as far as it depends on you, live at peace with everyone." We take the first step.

We take initiative. The Bible always puts the responsibility on us. This is the way of Jesus.

Next we take responsibility for the barriers on our side. We get the log out of our own eyes before we address others' issues. This usually means that we may need to ask for forgiveness. Two stories immediately come to mind.

I was in a closed-door meeting with Muslim and Christian leaders from around the world. During the dialogue, a veteran Mennonite peacemaker, David Shenk, said with humility and passion, "I am grieved over the Iraq war. Would you please forgive us?" The leader of the event from the Muslim side, Prince Ghazi of Jordan, was touched and later thanked Shenk publicly for his apology.

More recently, I went with the Vineyard Community Church of Gilbert (Arizona) to the Islamic Community Center of Phoenix for a Love Your Neighbor Dinner. During this gathering, both the imam and the pastor spoke about love of neighbor from their sacred texts. When Pastor Jack Moraine spoke, he said, "As followers of Jesus, we have failed to love you, our Muslim neighbors. Would you please forgive us?" You could have heard a pin drop in the mosque. The Muslims were visibly touched. All tensions in the air melted immediately, as Jack had modeled getting the log out of our own eyes.

As an important aside, it is easy to make public apologies that have no practical meaning. Native Americans, for example, are tired of white Americans apologizing and doing nothing to set things right. A true apology demands some form of evidence that one seeks to repent. In this case, showing up at the mosque to build relationships was the first step in Jack's repentance. Since that event, Jack and his church have reached out to Muslims in other practical ways.

Many Christians resist this kind of humility. Instead they wrongly want to begin with the peacemaking practice of rebuke. They want to focus on the logs in the Muslims' eyes. In so doing, they disobey the teaching of Jesus. They fail to follow the Prince of Peace. And opportunities to build bridges are lost.

Yes, there is a place to point out our grievances and differences with Muslims. Eventually we need to speak the truth in love to our Muslim neighbors. But that comes *after* we have pursued peace, taken responsibility for our own logs and reached out in love to our Muslim neighbors.[5]

How might social peacemaking work between the LGBT community and evangelicals? According to the research of David Kinnaman and Gabe Lyons, evangelicals not only oppose the gay lifestyle but also have a reputation for hostility toward gay people.[6] The animosity between the gay community and evangelicals rivals the animosity between Muslims and evangelicals.

How does Jesus' teaching on peacemaking apply to the LGBT community? I can imagine many of my conservative evangelical friends retorting immediately, "Why do we want to make peace with the gay community anyway? Homosexuality is sin."

But think about how Jesus related to sinners. He was accused of being their friend (Matthew 9:11; Luke 15:2). And in relating to sexual sinners—like the woman interrupting the Pharisee's party (Luke 7:36-50) or the woman caught in adultery (John 8:1-11)—Jesus demonstrated love. By contrast, Jesus' opponents, the Pharisees, were antagonistic toward sinners. They believed that they demonstrated love for God by hating sinners, that holiness manifested itself through hostility. Sadly, many evangelicals follow the way of the Pharisees but do so mistakenly in the name of Jesus.

It is worth repeating what I said earlier about Jesus: he taught and modeled exclusive truth claims and inclusive love aims. The Pharisees and many evangelicals zealously uphold the truth claims but do poorly in the love aims.

I confess it is sometimes hard to embrace both. And this is not just a theological or theoretical issue for me. A few years ago my oldest daughter, Kaleen, told us she was gay. This rocked our categories and caused some serious introspection. Kaleen had been a leader in her church youth group during high school and a leader in her college campus ministry.

This pushed us back to Jesus. Since the day I started following Jesus in 1970 till now, I have firmly upheld Jesus' truth claims. Now I am learning more about his inclusive love aims. Relating to the LGBT community like Jesus would has become personal.

Two friends of mine, both young Vineyard pastors, have adapted the material Peace Catalyst has developed on building bridges with Muslims and applied them to the gay community. Jim Pool, lead pastor of the Renaissance Vineyard in Ferndale, Michigan, took my book *Grace and Truth: Toward Christlike Relations with Muslims* and reworked it so it applies to the LGBT community. Jeff Cannell, lead pastor of the Central Vineyard in Columbus, Ohio, showed how each point in my peacemaking diagram (see figure 2.1) has relevance for reaching out to the gay community. I look forward to seeing what they learn and how God will use them.[7]

I don't have to believe what Muslims believe to love them, nor do I have to agree with the LGBT community to love them. I like how Brian Zahnd addresses these issues:

> I'm not sure it is helpful to automatically identify secularists, homosexuals and Muslims as enemies. But even if we do, the fact remains that Jesus calls us to love and bless our enemies, and not mock and revile them. Let's get this clear—loving the homosexual is no more an endorsement of homosexuality than Jesus' refusal to stone the adulterous woman was an endorsement of adultery. Because Jesus would not stone an adulterer did not mean Jesus was pro-adultery. Because Paul addressed the pagans of Athens respectfully did not mean Paul was pro-paganism.[8]

Therefore, social peacemaking between evangelicals and the LGBT community (or any other group, for that matter) follows the same steps mentioned above with the Muslim community. We do not begin with rebuke. Rather we take the initiative to reach out in love. Next we get the logs out of our own eyes. We show humility by asking for forgiveness for not loving our gay neighbors as ourselves.

We repent for the hatred and anger evangelicals have displayed toward gays.

It is common for evangelicals to say, "Love the sinner; hate the sin." I used to think this was a brilliant summary of Christian social ethics. As I have matured, I realize that there is something wrong with this seemingly balanced statement. I believe it does summarize how Jesus engages with all people. The problem is we aren't like Jesus. Jesus really did love everyone, and he hated all types of sin. But we pick and choose which sin to really hate. I have met *very* few evangelicals who take all the sins listed in Scripture seriously.[9] If we did, we would be much more humble.

So I think it is more accurate to say, "Love the sinner, and hate your own sin."[10] This is what it means practically to get the log out of our own eye. If we take our own sin seriously, we are able to speak the truth in love about our differing views of marriage and sexuality with the gay community.

Social peacemaking, like all peacemaking, is not just about methods; it is about our motives. If we do peacemaking to evangelize Muslims or do peacemaking to correct the LGBT community, our motives are most likely not right.

God commands us to pursue peace with everyone, not as a means to an end but as an end in itself. Peacemaking is a good deed that glorifies God. Here's another way of saying this: God commands us to love our neighbor without an ulterior motive. As Michael Gatlin, pastor of the Duluth (Minnesota) Vineyard, says, "Love God. Love people. Period."

PURSUING PEACE AND SHARING THE GOSPEL OF PEACE

What is an evangelical peacemaker? For many, this is an oxymoron. How can you be a true peacemaker and at the same time be a faithful evangelical? I get criticisms from both Muslims and Christians about this. Some Muslims accuse us of doing peacemaking only as a means to evangelize. Some Christians believe that peacemaking without evangelizing is meaningless. Is this really an either-or issue? Is there a tension between peacemaking and gospeling? There isn't for Pastor James of Nigeria.

> Pastor James was born in Kaduna, Nigeria. As a teenager, James joined the Christian Association of Nigeria, and at twenty-seven became general secretary of the Youth Wing. When fighting between Christians and Muslims broke out in Kaduna in 1987, James became the head of a Christian militia. He became adept at using Scripture to justify violence.
>
> When he was thirty-two, a fight broke out between Christians and Muslims over control of a market. The Christians were outnumbered, and twenty of them were killed. James passed out, and when he woke up, he found that his right arm had been chopped off with a machete.
>
> Imam Ashafa comes from a long line of Muslim scholars. In 1987, when religious violence hit Kaduna, like James, Ashafa became a militia leader. He says, "We planted the seed of genocide, and we used the scripture to do that. As a leader you create a scenario where this is the only interpretation."
>
> But Ashafa's mentor, a Sufi hermit, tried to warn the young man away from violence. In 1992, Christian militiamen stabbed the hermit to death and threw his body down a well. Ashafa's only mission became revenge: he was going to kill James. Then, one Friday during a sermon, Ashafa's imam told the story of when the Prophet Muhammad had gone to preach at Ta'if, a town about seventy miles southeast of Mecca. Bleeding after being stoned and cast out of town, Muhammad was visited by an angel who asked if he'd like those who mistreated him to be destroyed. Muhammad said no. "The imam was talking directly to me," Ashafa said. During the sermon, he began to cry. The next time he met James, he'd forgiven him entirely. To prove it, he went to visit James's sick mother in the hospital.

> Slowly the pastor and imam began to work together, but James was leery. "Ashafa carries the psychological mark. I carry the physical and psychological mark," he said. At a Christian conference in Nigeria, a fellow pastor pulled James aside and said, in almost the same words as the Sufi hermit had, "You can't preach Jesus with hate in your heart." James said, "That was my real turning point. I came back totally deprogrammed."
>
> For more than a decade now, James and Ashafa have traveled to Nigerian cities and to other countries where Christians and Muslims are fighting. They tell stories of how they manipulated religious texts to get young people into the streets to shed blood. Both still adhere strictly to their scriptures; they just read them more deeply and emphasize different verses.
>
> Sadly, the imam is frequently accused of being a sellout because he associates with Christians. He identifies himself very much as a fundamentalist and sees himself as one who emulates Muhammad. Although he and Pastor James don't discuss it, he also proselytizes among Christians. "I want James to die as a Muslim, and he wants me to die as a Christian. My Islam is proselytizing. It's about bringing the whole world to Islam."
>
> Such missionary zeal drives both men, infusing their struggle to rise above their history of conflict. Pastor James still believes strongly in salvation in Christ alone: "Jesus said, 'I am the way and the truth and the life.' He still challenges Christians to rely on the strict and literal word, and he's still uncompromising on fundamental issues of Christianity."[11]

James, the evangelical pastor, partnered with Ashafa, the Muslim imam, to do social peacemaking in conflict-ridden Nigeria. Their commitment to partnering for peace does not mean they have dissolved their distinctive, historic beliefs into one religion. Rather, it means they each seek to be authentically faithful to their historic beliefs and find within those beliefs the resources to reach out to one another in love and respect. Both men work for true peace. Both men boldly share their faith. Both are peacemakers without compromise.

I was talking about Peace Catalyst International at a meeting when a woman exclaimed, "But if people don't come to Christ, everything else is worthless!" Really? Worthless? What is the relationship between peacemaking and sharing the good news? How do followers of Jesus live out the ministry of reconciliation?

When we began Peace Catalyst International, Pastor Tyler Johnson of Redemption Church, a network of churches in Arizona, encouraged me with these wise words: "Rick, evangelical peacemaking is like evangelical relief and development. Groups like World Vision commit themselves to quality relief and development in the name of Christ. Of course they want to bear witness to Christ. But they want to do their work with excellence, unto to the Lord whether someone comes to Christ or not. Evangelical peacemaking is like evangelical relief and development."

In the same vein, Christians have started hospitals around the world because they believe that God called them to heal the sick. We do so even if every sick person doesn't come to Christ. To care for the sick is not worthless, and in many ways it is a demonstration of the gospel and can prepare people to receive the gospel.

I have argued that peacemaking is multidimensional in that we call people to peace with God and neighbor. It is also comprehensive: the physical and spiritual dimensions of life are integrated. And the good news is holistic—about both personal reconciliation and social transformation. We share the gospel of peace, and we pursue the peace of God. Ideally peacemaking and sharing the good news are integrated.

In practice, however, peacemaking and sharing the good news don't always go together. There are times when someone is reconciled to God but fails to reconcile with his neighbor. People like this need further teaching and encouragement to "obey all that Jesus commanded." This is one reason Peace Catalyst International has seminars about interpersonal peacemaking. There are far too many professing followers of Christ who fail to make peace with their neighbors, much less their enemies.

There are other instances when making peace between neighbors enables us to bear witness to Jesus effectively. People are drawn to the goodness of the gospel when they see our lights shine in this way. They want to know about the good news of God's reconciling love in Christ. And they decide to follow Jesus.

Sometimes, however, people rejoice in the peace made between them and their neighbors but do not want to follow the Prince of Peace. In this case, the good deed of peacemaking still finds favor with God. For Jesus said, "Let your light shine before others, that they may see your good deeds and glorify your Father in heaven" (Matthew 5:16). The good deed of peacemaking glorifies God and brings a piece of the kingdom to earth. That is not worthless!

PEACEMAKING, EVANGELISM AND THE MIDDLE EASTERN PRINCE

The relationship between working for peace and sharing the gospel of peace is crucial. And our motives are profoundly important. Because of this, I think it will be helpful to share some email correspondence I recently had with a peacemaking prince of a Middle Eastern country. He accused me of doing peacemaking as an evangelistic strategy. Here's how I responded:

> I understand your concern, caution and even consternation with evangelicals. I also realize that my past role as international director of Frontiers makes it hard for you to trust me. But if you want me to be honest with you, I stepped down from that role in 2007 because I could no longer live out my faith like a traditional evangelical.
>
> That's why I loved the last paragraph in your email. I am touched by the idea of focusing on my own personal conversion. God has been challenging me about this. Thank you

for sharing that. May our relationship reflect the affection described in the Qur'an.[12]

Thanks too for your incisive questions. Even though I no longer see myself as a traditional evangelical, I still want to live and share the good news. God commands me to both love my neighbor and share my faith. For me this means that the Great Commandment governs the Great Commission. In other words, I need to love my neighbor with "no strings attached"—whether they want to hear the gospel or not.

For example, when someone wants to join my organization (Peace Catalyst International—PCI), we question them thoroughly about the issues you raise. We make it clear that too many evangelicals love their neighbor or do peacemaking in order to bear witness (or try to convert people). We call this "bait and switch." We tell them that they should not join PCI with that kind of attitude. God commands us to love our neighbor without an ulterior motive or another agenda. As one of my pastor friends says, "Love God. Love people. Period."

So to be totally honest with you: before God, I cannot answer your questions with a simple yes or no. If I am to be faithful to Scripture, I must be a both-and thinker and doer. I please God when I love my neighbor without any other agenda. So with all my heart I strive to do that. But you asked me what I desire. I desire to love with a pure heart and I desire to share my faith as well.

During an interfaith leadership team meeting, a mainline Christian pastor named John (non-evangelical) asked me why I was involved. He knew I was evangelical and feared that I only wanted to convert people. I shared what I said above. Then Imam Ahmad interrupted us, "Pastor John, why does that bother you? In the seven resolutions document we have agreed on, we acknowledge that I want you to embrace Islam and you want me to accept Jesus as my Lord and Savior."[13]

> I have more in common with Imam Ahmad than I do with Pastor John. Both Ahmad and I believed we could pursue peace together and still bear witness to our respective faiths. I realize that you have a different viewpoint from this imam. But as I learned from you in the Amman Message, there is great diversity of opinion in Ịslam.[14] There are many imams like Ahmad and an increasing number of evangelicals like me who are serious about peace. I hope we can work more closely *with people like you.*

The prince was not convinced, and he still struggles with evangelicals. But to his credit he pointed out one possible way we may be able to work together in the future: "insha Allah" (God willing).

9

HOW PEACE CATALYSTS SPREAD THE PEACE

PART TWO: SIX SPHERES OF PEACEMAKING

Church history reveals that Jesus' message of enemy-love and non-violent peacemaking was deeply needed but rarely heeded.

BRUXY CAVEY

I had a stimulating conversation recently with a fellow peacemaker. I was enjoying the conversation when out of nowhere he made a joke about beauty queens talking about "world peace" as if this were dumb. In the past I would have chuckled along with him. But this time his comment rankled me. I didn't chuckle.

World peace is no joke. Beauty queens who want world peace are not silly—naive, maybe, but not silly. They voice what most of us yearn for deep down inside: peace. And it is God who puts that desire in us.

The magnitude of our peace calling is huge. And many of us miss it. I missed it. In fact, I am embarrassed to say that in my first book on peacemaking, I didn't even address what it means to love your enemy. But God has opened my mind and changed my heart. Part of this conversion centered on three biblical commands, which I've mentioned previously but are worth repeating. They describe peacemaking without borders:

- "If it is possible, as far as it depends on you, live at peace with everyone" (Romans 12:18).
- "Live in peace with everyone" (Hebrews 12:14).
- "Love your enemies" (Matthew 5:44).

Let me share how God has led me in my peace pilgrimage. The two figures in this chapter, "Peacemaking Continuum" and "Peacemaking Spheres," help me visualize the big picture of God's peacemaking purposes. They can guide the busy pastor, scholar or activist in building a peace ministry.

PEACEMAKING CONTINUUM

Imagine God's work of peacemaking as a continuum. We experience God's peace through Christ. This results in peace with ourselves as we receive increased healing in our own lives. Jesus then leads us to live this out with his people, with our neighbors and ultimately with our enemies.[1]

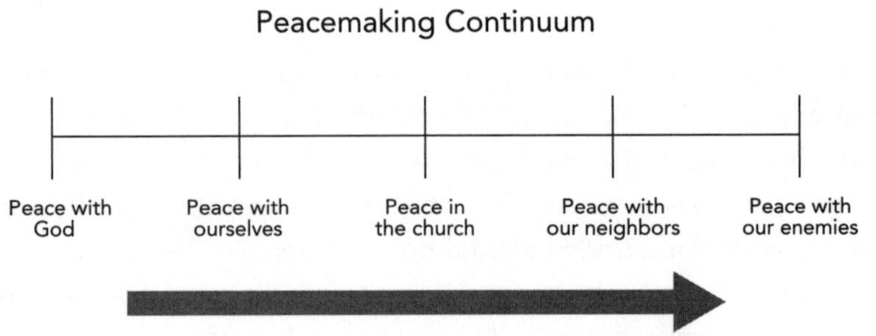

Peacemaking Continuum

Peace with God
Peace with ourselves
Peace in the church
Peace with our neighbors
Peace with our enemies

Figure 9.1

Ideally, the church does peacemaking simultaneously in all five points on the peacemaking continuum. Evangelism and all forms of witness lead people to peace with God. Counseling, spiritual direction and prayer for inner healing help people find peace with themselves. Most churches have specific ministries and formally appointed people to help others find peace with God and peace with themselves.

But few churches have specific ministries or formally appoint people to do peacemaking in the church, with neighbors or with enemies. It is assumed that the pastor or other church leaders will handle the role of peacemaker. While church leaders do peacemaking (and some do it well), many are not trained in it and fail to provide training for their congregation. But note that the five points on this spectrum are something that *every* believer needs to do.

What would happen if evangelicals were proactive in their approach to peace as Jesus commanded? What would it look like if evangelicals lived out a peace ethic consistently—in all areas of their lives? What would happen if the evangelical view of peace was as comprehensive as the Bible's? In 2012, one hundred peacemakers, scholars and activists gathered at Georgetown University in Washington D.C., to wrestle with these very issues at Evangelicals for Peace: A Summit on Christian Moral Responsibility in the 21st Century.[2] During this summit I shared about the Six Spheres of Peacemaking and how they relate to the church universal. It is something that God's people from around the globe are involved in.

SIX SPHERES OF PEACEMAKING

As you can see in figure 9.2, the six spheres are personal, interpersonal, social, urban, national and international. Each of these is biblical, each builds on and encompasses the previous sphere, and each is more complex than the former. The following typology describes my understanding of the scope of peacemaking for evangelicals.

1. Personal peace (between God, self and others, resulting in peace within oneself). We experience peace with God when we enter into relationship with him through Christ. The gospel is explicitly described as the gospel of peace five times in the New Testament (Acts

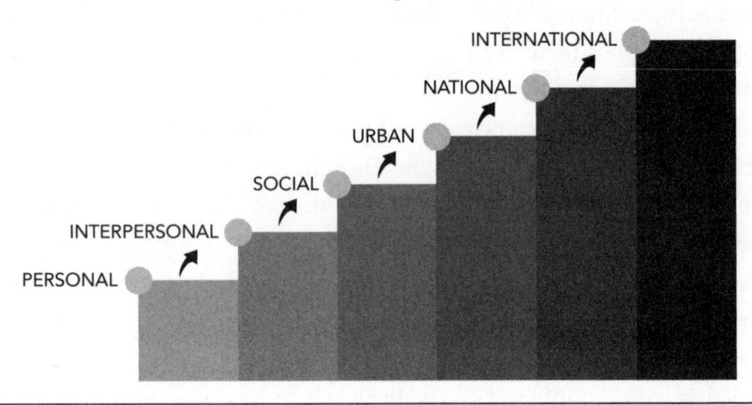

Figure 9.2

10:36; Ephesians 2:13-17; 6:15; Colossians 1:20; Romans 5:1). Thus, sharing the gospel of peace is one way we help people experience personal peace. Personal peace also comes through the practice of spiritual disciplines, especially as we pray, walk by faith and live in peace with others (Philippians 4:6-7; Romans 15:13; Ephesians 4:3; Colossians 3:15).

2. ***Interpersonal peace (between individuals).*** We experience interpersonal peace as we proactively pursue peace with other individuals by taking responsibility for our wrongdoings, accepting reproof, asking for forgiveness, reproving those who have wronged us and forgiving them (Matthew 5:23-24; 7:3-5; 18:15-17; Luke 17:3-4; Ephesians 4:32; Colossians 3:13).

3. ***Social peace (between groups).*** Conflicts between groups often arise out of cultural, racial or religious differences, which then lead to prejudice, fear, hatred and misunderstanding. Again, some of the most prominent group conflicts include gender conflict, class conflict, religious conflict, racial conflict and conflicts over sexual orientation. The commands to pursue peace and love one's enemy provide the foundation for social peacemaking (Romans 12:18; Hebrews 12:14; Matthew 5:44).

*4. **Urban peace (in cities).*** Urbanization is one of the defining traits of the modern world; over half of the world population now lives in cities. Jeremiah described a relevant paradigm for urban ministry: "Seek the welfare of the city where I have sent you into exile, and pray to the LORD on its behalf; for in its welfare [shalom] you will have welfare [shalom]" (Jeremiah 29:7 NASB).

Urban peace—seeking the shalom of the city—is broader and more complex than interpersonal or social peace. It includes peace with God, social harmony, health, economic prosperity and human flourishing.[3] God called the Jewish exiles to seek the common good of the cities where they lived. In New Testament terms, God was calling them to be salt and light, to glorify God through their loving deeds of service to those outside of the faith (Matthew 5:13-16). Urban peace involves working with the government and all types of organizations for the common good of the city. It is a comprehensive and multidimensional peacemaking approach to the city.[4]

*5. **National peace (within a nation).*** Most of today's wars are civil wars, not international wars. Countries like Sudan, Somalia, Nigeria and the Philippines immediately come to mind. These national conflicts usually have a variety of triggers. Weak, corrupt or oppressive government, ethnic diversity, religious diversity, human rights violations and poverty are the most common. Even though many of these clashes begin as national conflicts, they often escalate and spill over into surrounding nations—endangering their security and resulting in complex humanitarian emergencies. So a national peace problem often becomes an international peace problem.

But even in nations where no wars are going on, significant conflict takes place and peacemaking becomes necessary. Making peace at the national level encompasses urban peacemaking practices along with robust political engagement. The church needs to find formal and informal ways to influence the state.

*6. **International peace (between or involving the nations).*** Peacemaking at this level usually involves complex interaction between international, regional and local actors to mitigate, manage or resolve conflict. This is often referred to as multitrack diplomacy.[5] Track one focuses on top leaders, usually with government-to-government interaction. The United Nations and other international and regional organizations are also involved at this level. Track two focuses on middle-level leaders or nonstate actors, such as international non-government organizations, faith-based organizations, schools and private businesses. Track three refers to grassroots leaders, those considered to be indigenous peacemakers and local actors. Formal mediation tends to be the most common method of peacemaking, especially at a track-one level.[6] The Common Word dialogue at Yale University would be an example of track-two international peacemaking.[7] Peace Catalyst International does some track-three work by getting pastors and imams together over a meal, for example.

Few individuals are called to embrace or practice peace in a comprehensive manner. Thus it is more accurate to say that the six spheres of peacemaking describe the role of the whole church—the church universal. God's people from around the globe engage in all six of these spheres, depending on their calling. Nevertheless, God calls individuals to grow in their practice of peace, which means that God will often lead us into other spheres.

Jesus' teaching on peace may begin in our hearts and our homes. But it pushes us beyond our comfort zones and outside the walls of our churches to our neighbors and even our enemies. It overflows to our cities, states and nation. It encompasses global conflict and foreign policy—peacemaking without borders.

So, what does peacemaking without borders look like in the real world? No one could have predicted some of the amazing peace breakthroughs that have taken place during my lifetime.[8] Some of these peace movements were led by Christians, while others were at least influenced by Christians or Christian principles. Here are five out of the many prominent events that demonstrate the power of nonviolent resistance, highlighting social, national and international peacemaking.

- The civil rights movement in the United States, led by Martin Luther King Jr., outlawed racial discrimination against black Americans and restored their voting rights.
- People Power in the Philippines was a series of nonviolent and prayerful mass street demonstrations that toppled the brutal dictator Ferdinand Marcos.
- The fall of the Berlin Wall in 1989 marked the end of the Cold War and the collapse of communism.
- The dismantling of apartheid in South Africa, after decades of cruel oppression, took place under the leadership of Nelson Mandela and Desmond Tutu.
- The end of a fourteen-year civil war in Liberia and the toppling of the ruthless dictator Charles Taylor happened when Christian and Muslim women partnered under the leadership of Leymah Gbowee.

But the work of shalom making is not just about momentous occasions like the peace breakthroughs above. Here's an example of urban peacemaking on a much smaller scale.

> In 1998 serious conflict broke out between Christians and Muslims in the city of Solo, in Central Java. Consequently, the religious leaders formed an interreligious peace committee to rebuild trust and work toward concord. A young pastor on this committee says that on his first visit to the Hizbullah[9] command center, the commander greeted him gruffly, saying "You are a Christian and an infidel, and therefore I can kill you!" Unfazed, the pastor returned again and again to drink tea and talk.
>
> Then the pastor invited the commander and his officers to fly with several Christian leaders to Banda Aceh to work with Christian teams in the post-tsunami reconstruction. Remarkably, the Hizbullah leaders accepted, and for two weeks they worked with the Christian teams in rebuilding projects. The commander slept in the same room with the pastor, and they became friends.

He confided in the pastor, "I have discovered that you Christians are good infidels."

Afterward they met again for further peacemaking talks. They had invited David Shenk to speak to the group and offered to translate the book he coauthored with Badru Kateregga, titled *A Muslim and a Christian in Dialogue* (1997). When the pastor handed the book to the commander, the commander broke down. When he regained his composure, he said, "I am overcome, for this book is revealing another way, the way of peacefully sharing faith instead of violently confronting one another."

When asked about his evangelism, the pastor says, "My calling is to bear witness, mostly through praxis, to the reconciling love of Christ. I give account of my faith in Jesus to all who ask. Conversion is not my responsibility; that is the work of God." Remarkably his church has grown from forty to 250 in the last dozen years, and with the advocacy of Hizbullah, they are planning to build a second church in Solo.

When asked how the transformation in relationships took place, the pastor replied, "Lots of cups of tea—and the Holy Spirit!"[10]

Most peacemaking breakthroughs take place interpersonally, between individuals. Peacemakers who bear fruit interpersonally have learned to cultivate the habits of ordinary peaceful existence: walking in personal peace, showing hospitality, listening well, learning to ask good questions, speaking the truth in love, refusing to hold grudges and forgiving from the heart. Success in making peace often revolves around one conversation at a time.[11]

As my daughters were growing up, we would often talk about "shalom in the home." We worked hard at instilling peacemaking practices in our girls and between all of us. We taught and modeled the importance of forgiveness. Nevertheless, my family has had more than its share of conflict and problems.

I am happy to say, though, that most of the time we are all peacemakers. As my oldest daughter, Kaleen, said, "Dad, all of us take initiative in our relationships. If there is conflict or problems, we are the ones who usually reach out to our friends or acquaintances." I have seen this over and over again with our daughters. And I am proud of them.

Recently, conflict cropped up in our family again when Kaleen told us she was gay. Since that day in 2008, Fran's and my relationship with her has been rocky. It took time, but Kaleen and I have worked through our differences and made amends. Our relationship is improving all the time. But Kaleen really struggled in her relationship with Fran. She felt like her mom didn't accept or really love her. Kaleen had also grown distant from her two sisters. Our family was fragmenting, and we needed to do something about it.

After much soul searching, prayer and encouragement from me, Fran phoned Kaleen. (Since we live in different states, we need to phone rather than talk face to face.) She began to talk about the painful words and events that had alienated Kaleen. Both women shared from their heart in a new way. But there was no reconciliation. In anger and out of hurt, Kaleen said adamantly, "Mom, you have never accepted me and never loved me." The conversation ended. Relationships frayed.

Kaleen shared what happened with her partner, who listened attentively and then challenged Kaleen about her exaggeration: "You never felt unconditional love from your mother? You can't use words like *never*, Kaleen. Your mom obviously loves you." As a peacemaker, she encouraged Kaleen to share her feelings but also to use her words more accurately. This led to continued conversations that began to heal hurts and mend the relationship.

At the same time, our youngest daughter, Jessica, decided to intervene. She called Kaleen and said something like this: "You know that Tessa and I are close and have ostracized you from the family. You were the busy and important big sister, and we were young brats. But we are growing up, and we think family is important now. It's sad that we are so distant. Dad, Mom, Tessa and I have worked through our issues and have grown close. We want you back in the family. Why don't you come and visit us? Let's get to know each other as adults. I want us to become a close family."

God used me, Kaleen's partner and Jessica to build bridges and make peace. Kaleen visited her sisters and has been on the phone with all of us regularly. Fran has visited Kaleen and begun to work through their issues. There is a new sense of warmth and affection in our relationships. In fact, we are the closest we've ever been. We are experiencing shalom in the home anew. But true shalom is never a one-time event or achievement. We are on a lifelong journey—together.

How can we follow the Prince of Peace into a world of conflict? The famous Old Testament prophecy about the Prince of Peace gives us enduring hope and a necessary perspective:

> For to us a child is born, to us a son is given, and the government will be on his shoulders. And he will be called Wonderful Counselor, Mighty God, Everlasting Father, Prince of Peace. Of the increase of his government and peace there will be no end. He will reign on David's throne and over his kingdom, establishing and upholding it with justice and righteousness from that time on and forever. The zeal of the LORD Almighty will accomplish this. (Isaiah 9:6-7)

Jesus is the promised Prince of Peace. His kingdom will be a kingdom of shalom. His peace will be a comprehensive peace (including justice and righteousness). His peace will be multidimensional (peace with God, social harmony, welfare, health, prosperity and human flourishing). His peace movement is expanding and will endure forever.

God is on a mission to bring peace to earth. And he will be successful. For Isaiah said, "The zeal of the LORD Almighty will accomplish this" (9:7). He will accomplish his peace purposes through people like you and me.

So let's listen to Jesus' commission afresh and receive it as his commission to us in the present:

> On the evening of that first day of the week, when the disciples were together, with the doors locked for fear of the Jewish leaders, Jesus came and stood among them and said, "Peace be with you!" After he said this, he showed them his hands and side. The disciples were overjoyed when they saw the Lord. Again Jesus said, "Peace be with you! As the Father has sent me, I am sending you." (John 20:19-21)

Jesus commissions us to imitate him in the world. He sends us as his peace catalysts with a *double* blessing of peace. This blessing summarizes the essence of his work, the gospel of peace, and points us to his promises of peace:

> Peace I leave with you; my peace I give you. I do not give to you as the world gives. Do not let your hearts be troubled and do not be afraid. (John 14:27)

> I have told you these things, so that in me you may have peace. In this world you will have trouble. But take heart! I have overcome the world. (John 16:33)

Jesus reminded us that he is the source of peace: "*My peace* I give to you," "*in me* you . . . have peace." His peace is not the absence of anxiety or trouble. Rather it enables us to remain calm and confident in the midst of conflict. Jesus' peace anchors us in the storms of life.

So feel his personal peace and follow the Prince of Peace. Resolve conflict. Restore harmony. Spread the peace and share the gospel of peace.

Together we can ignite a peace movement. That's what peace catalysts do.

APPENDIX A

IDEAS FOR JOINING GOD IN HIS PEACE MISSION

How can you cultivate and embody what it means to be a peacemaker? What would have to happen for you to become part of a peacemaking community? If you're interested in further hands-on training through a seminar for your church or organization, contact Peace Catalyst International. We do peacemaking seminars on interpersonal peacemaking for churches and especially for leadership teams in churches. We also put on peacemaking seminars focused primarily on the social aspects of peacemaking—"engaging the other." Contact Peace Catalyst International through our website, peace-catalyst.net, or contact me directly at ricklove@peace-catalyst.net.

If God has spoken to you about the importance of seeking "the peace and prosperity of the city" (Jeremiah 29:7),[1] check out churches that model this practice well. Redeemer Presbyterian Church in New York City, led by Tim Keller, has an explicit goal to "seek to renew the city spiritually, socially and culturally." One example is their Hope for New York program, which provides volunteer and financial resources to organizations serving the poor and marginalized (for example, immigrants, the homeless, those living with HIV/AIDS). They partner with more than thirty nonprofit organizations to bring shalom to New York. (For more information on this church, visit redeemer.com.)

Columbus Vineyard in Columbus, Ohio, led by Rich Nathan, is another great example. They have a huge community center that offers afterschool programs, free health clinics, citizenship classes, sports programs, financial counseling and so much more. Their mission is "to transform the city of Columbus by love and good deeds for the glory of God, extending the truth, power and love of the Gospel to build friendships with our city, one life at a time." You can find out more about Vineyard Columbus and its programs by visiting vineyard columbus.org.

And, finally, you need to commit yourself to Jesus' brand of peacemaking. One way to do this is to read through the Peace Catalyst Manifesto (appendix C) and sign it as an act of faith. You can also visit peace-catalyst.net/join-the-movement.

APPENDIX B

SEVEN STEPS TO LOVING REPROOF

Here is a practical tool for you to review when you face conflict.

- *Prepare your heart.* Ask the Lord to fill you with his love for the offender. This is not a nice "devotional" suggestion. This is a necessity for Jesus' brand of peacemaking. Reconciliation is an act of love.
- *Prepare your words.* Your preparation will take time, yet your initial comments should be said in one minute or less. I either write or rehearse in my head the points I want to cover in the initial conversation. Here are some of the main points that you need to address:
  - Begin on a positive note. If possible, try to affirm the person before confronting. This is what Jesus did with the churches in the book of Revelation 2–3. For example, "Susan, I really appreciate how well you organize the meeting. Thanks for your hard work in putting it on. I am concerned about one thing that you said during the meeting and wanted to talk to you about it." (Note: If you rarely affirm the person, don't suddenly do it now. It will be seen as insincere, as a form of flattery or as manipulation.)
  - You can also begin by asking questions. "Hey John, you seemed distant and angry the other day. Is everything all right? Have I offended you in some way?"
  - Name the issue as concretely as possible, and give an example of

  when it happened. "Jim, you were complaining about your boss the other day and yet never talked to him about your concerns. I know you are frustrated, but this is gossip."

  - Describe your emotions about this issue. Don't use an accusatory word like "You!" Instead say, "I felt _________ when you did this." "I feel uneasy when I hear you gossip about your boss, Jim, because I wonder what you may be saying behind my back."
  - Clarify why this is important. "Gossip hurts team morale and does not help us solve problems."
  - Identify your contribution to the problem. "Jim, I am sorry I did not talk to you sooner about this. I shouldn't have let this go as long as I did."
  - Indicate your desire to resolve the issue. "Jim, I will do whatever I can to help you work this through with your boss. Let me know when you plan on sharing with him, and I will pray. I would be willing to mediate between you if necessary."[1]

- *Find the right time and place.* Privacy is important in conflict resolution. "If a brother or sister sins, go and point out the fault, just between the two of you" (Matthew 18:15). Timing is also important: "It is wonderful to say the right thing at the right time!" (Proverbs 15:23 NLT). So manage the location of the meeting and when you meet. Find a place where you will not be interrupted and when the person will be fresh.
- *Stick to the facts.* You don't know people's motives. We often get offended because we think they did it intentionally to hurt us or others.
- *Focus on the problem, not the person.* What is the action that offended you? In doing mediation in the workplace, we encourage people to write up the business problem. For example, "John usually comes late to our meetings and is not prepared for them." That is very different from saying, "John is a bad person."

- *Invite the person to respond.* This is where the heart of the dialogue takes place. Listen carefully to what she says. Don't get defensive. Sympathize with her feelings, ask clarifying questions as needed, and keep the conversation focused on the issue at hand. Don't get sidetracked.
- *End with resolution.* Come to an agreement about what has been said and what will happen next: "What is needed for resolution? How can we move forward from here? Has anything been left unsaid that needs to be said? What more can I do from my end to show my support for our relationship?"

APPENDIX C

THE PEACE CATALYST MANIFESTO

In a world rife with conflict, we resolve to follow the peaceable ways of Jesus the Messiah. God's true children work for peace. We confess we have often overlooked the biblical mandate to pursue peace. Sometimes we have shared the tenets of our faith without exhibiting the character of its Founder. Thus, by the grace of God, we commit ourselves to peacemaking—to resolve conflict and restore harmony as God commands. We commit ourselves anew to this mandate within our homes, across our religious communities, throughout our spheres of influence and among the nations of the world.

Conflict and prejudice have affected all our relationships and every dimension of our lives. For this reason, God's plan for the lives of his people is to produce comprehensive reconciliation. This includes reconciliation with God; racial, class and gender reconciliation; and reconciliation to the entire creation. Thus we resolve to pursue multidimensional reconciliation—peace in all relationships and in all spheres of life.

We recognize that peacemaking is not always the same as reconciliation. Peacemaking refers to loving initiatives that seek to break down barriers and overcome hostility between people or peoples, whether or not there is reconciliation. But reconciliation is the ultimate goal of all peacemaking.

As peacemakers, we recognize that we are bearers of shalom, the ancient biblical concept that encompasses peace, welfare, health, prosperity and human flourishing. Shalom highlights the multidimensional nature of true peace, which includes the spiritual, relational, economic and environmental dimensions of life. Thus we resolve to pursue peace holistically.

We will seek to find fellow peacemakers to start reconciling communities (we also call these "communities of reconciliation"). As members of a reconciling community, we promise to follow these *eight pillars of reconciliation:*

1. We will pray for peace (2 Thessalonians 3:16; 1 Timothy 2:1-2).
2. We will make every effort to be at peace with all people (Romans 12:18; Ephesians 4:3; Hebrews 12:14).
3. We will take responsibility for our part in conflict. We will take the log out of our own eyes as Jesus taught (Matthew 7:3-5).
4. We will lovingly challenge or reprove those who sin (Matthew 5:23-24; 18:15; Galatians 6:1).
5. We will accept reproof (Proverbs 12:1, 15).
6. We will ask for forgiveness when we sin and when we are reproved (Luke 17:3-4).
7. We will forgive those who sin against us (Matthew 6:14-15; 18:35).
8. We will love our enemies (Matthew 5:44-45; Luke 6:27-36).

Signed ______________________________

Date ________________________________

Print Name __________________________

Email _______________________________

You can watch the PCI Manifesto slide show on YouTube: www.youtube.com/watch?v=Bqg4s_QcsLE.

APPENDIX D

THE GRACE AND TRUTH AFFIRMATION

The following, "Full of Grace and Truth: Toward Christlike Relationships with Muslims," describes Peace Catalyst International's commitment to the social dimension of peacemaking. You can read more about this at http://peace-catalyst.net/training/grace--truth.

Jesus was full of grace and truth (John 1:14). As his followers, we aspire to walk in the fullness of grace and truth in our relationships with Muslims. We seek to be agents of peace in a polarized world.

Together Christians and Muslims make up over half of the human race. Thus, peaceful relations between these faith communities stand as one of the central challenges of this century. But the pathway to peace faces troublesome obstacles.

The relationship between Christians and Muslims is supercharged by the so-called "war on terror" and exacerbated by the fact that Western countries are perceived as "Christian" by many Muslims. The threat of terrorism, negative stereotypes of Muslims and ignorance have caused the church to shrink back from obeying the fundamental biblical commands to love and bear witness.

Moreover, just as there is significant theological, cultural and ideological diversity among Christians, so too is there among Muslims. The spectrum of Muslim perspectives and practices ranges from secularists, modernists, traditionalists and fundamentalists to a minuscule minority of violent extremists.

It has been our privilege to enjoy warm hospitality and deep interaction with Muslims around the world. They are neighbors, friends and colleagues who have challenged, clarified and encouraged our thinking about peacemaking.

In honor of Jesus Christ, the Prince of Peace, Peace Catalyst International affirms ten biblical guidelines that will enable Jesus' followers to serve as his representatives in relationship with Muslims of every persuasion. The following guidelines grow out of the Grace and Truth Project, reflecting Peace Catalyst's revised, personalized version of these affirmations.

- Be Jesus-centered in our interaction
- Be truthful and gracious in our words and witness
- Be wise in our words and witness
- Be respectful and bold in our witness
- Be prudent in our glocalized world
- Be persistent in our call for religious freedom
- Be peaceable and uncompromising in our dialogue
- Be loving toward all
- Differentiate between the role of church and state
- Support and challenge the state

1. Be Jesus-Centered in Our Interaction

Our focus is Jesus because he is the heart of the gospel. We say as Paul did, "For I resolved to know nothing while I was with you except Jesus Christ and him crucified" (1 Corinthians 2:2). We affirm a Jesus-centered approach to Muslims because it highlights the treasure of the gospel. It does not confuse the good news with Christendom, patriotism or our civilization.

Therefore, we seek to keep Jesus at the center of our lives, conversations and relationships with Muslims.

2. Be Truthful and Gracious in Our Words and Witness

We seek to be accurate when we speak about Muslims and their faith. Overstatement, exaggeration and words taken out of context should not be found among followers of Jesus, for he calls us to be careful about the words we speak (Matthew 12:36). God commands us not to bear false witness against our neighbor (Exodus 20:16) and to do unto others as we would have them do unto us (Matthew 7:12). Thus we strive to speak truthfully about Muslims, to respect Muslims' own interpretation of themselves and not to compare the best interpretation and practice of our faith with the worst interpretation and practice of theirs.

The content of our message is important, and so is the manner in which we convey it. As those who have received grace, we are to convey grace (Ephesians 4:29). Paul says, "Let your conversation be always full of grace . . . so that you may know how to answer everyone" (Colossians 4:6). The Bible calls us to truthful accuracy and fullness of grace.

Therefore, we seek to be accurate and positive in our witness. We also seek to be gracious in our communication, using kind words, even when we need to speak "hard" truths.

3. Be Wise in Our Words and Witness

God's Word calls us to walk in wisdom and to share our faith wisely. "Conduct yourselves with wisdom toward outsiders, making the most of the opportunity" (Colossians 4:5 NASB). What does wisdom look like in practice?

According to James, "the wisdom that comes from heaven is first of all pure; then peace-loving, considerate, submissive, full of mercy and good fruit, impartial and sincere. Peacemakers who sow in peace reap a harvest of righteousness" (James 3:17-18). Peace is the ruling idea in this passage. Heavenly wisdom creates a peacemaking community.

Therefore, we seek to walk in God's peace-producing wisdom.

4. Be Respectful and Bold in Our Witness

In the spirit of the Prince of Peace, respectful witness focuses on giving a positive presentation of the gospel. It does not attack the other or avoid presenting truth. As the apostle Peter said, "In your hearts revere Christ as Lord. Always be prepared to give an answer to everyone who asks you to give the reason for the hope that you have. But do this with gentleness and respect" (1 Peter 3:15 NIV). Numerous biblical examples invite us to emulate the boldness of early followers of Jesus in sharing the good news (such as Acts 4:31; 9:27-28; 13:46; 14:3; 17:30-31; 19:8).

Therefore, in obedience to the Scripture, we seek to be both respectful and bold in our witness.

5. Be Prudent in Our Glocalized World[1]

In the past, what we spoke to our community stayed in our community. But due to the Internet today, our words ricochet around the world, for good or for bad. When we try to explain who we are, what we believe, what we do and why we do it, our words may reach beyond our primary audience and enter the global marketplace of ideas. After saying something hurtful (whether intentional or not), we may try to clarify our statement. But the damage is already done. Conversely, when we say something positive, the kindness of our words may extend way beyond the circle of our community. Words are powerful.

Therefore, we seek to be prudent in our communication. "A truly wise person uses few words" (Proverbs 17:27 NLT).

6. Be Persistent in Our Call for Religious Freedom

We affirm the right of religious freedom for every person and community. We defend the right of Muslims to express their faith respectfully among Christians and of Christians to express their faith respectfully among Muslims. Moreover, we affirm the right of Muslims and Christians alike to change religious beliefs, practices and/or affiliations according to their conscience (2 Corinthians 4:2). Thus we stand against all forms of religious persecution toward Muslims, Christians or anyone else.

We concur with Pastor John Piper's incisive rationale for this perspective:

> Christians are tolerant of other faiths not because there is no absolute truth or that all faiths are equally valuable, but because

the one who is Absolute Truth, Jesus Christ, forbids the spread of his truth by the sword. Christian tolerance is the commitment that keeps lovers of competing faiths from killing each other. Christian tolerance is the principle that puts freedom above forced conversion, because it's rooted in the conviction that forced conversion is no conversion at all. Freedom to preach, to teach, to publish, to assemble for worship—these convictions flow from the essence of the Christian faith.[2]

Therefore, we strive to protect religious freedom for all.

7. Be Peaceable and Uncompromising in Our Dialogue

Dialogue between Muslims and Christians provides us with opportunities to understand Muslims, build relationships, engage in peacemaking and share an accurate explanation of our faith. Through dialogue we seek to reframe the Muslim-Christian relationship so it is no longer perceived as a "clash of civilizations."

But this does not mean we dissolve our distinctive, historic beliefs into an imaginary "one world religion." Rather, it means each community seeks to be authentically faithful to their historic beliefs and finds *within* those beliefs the resources to reach out to one another in love.

Therefore, we strive to work toward mutual respect, graciously bearing witness to our faith and working toward religious freedom.

8. Be Loving toward All

The world's Muslims are our neighbors, as Jesus used the term (Luke 10:29-37). The command of God to his people stands for all time: "Love your neighbor as yourself" (Leviticus 19:18; Luke 10:27). How can a follower of Christ take seriously Jesus' command to love our neighbor and, at the same time, address the real threat of terrorism by those who position themselves as our enemies? Jesus' teaching about love of enemy (Luke 6:35) is among the most radical and most ignored commands in the Bible. We do not want to engage in the "hermeneutics of evasion"—figuring out ways to interpret

Jesus' command so it doesn't apply to our lives.

Both peacemakers and those who love their enemies are described as "children of God" (Matthew 5:9; Luke 6:35). They are called children of God because they are acting like their Father: the God of Peace (Philippians 4:9; 1 Thessalonians 5:23). In other words, peacemakers and those who love their enemies demonstrate their authenticity as children of God by their words and acts of peace. Jesus modeled this by loving us and laying down his life for us, "while we were enemies" (Romans 5:10 NSAB; see also Colossians 1:21). After his enemies nailed him to the cross, he prayed, "Father, forgive them, for they do not know what they are doing" (Luke 23:34).

Therefore, we aspire to demonstrate the gospel with self-giving, sacrificial love toward our Muslim neighbors and toward the small minority of Muslims who might position themselves as our enemies.

9. Differentiate between the Role of Church and State

In Romans 12:9–13:10, Paul described a godly response to evil. He portrayed a sharp contrast between how God's people are to respond to evil versus how the government should respond.

Jesus' followers are called to a peacemaking ethic of sacrificial love. Paul began the section with an appeal to love (Romans 12:9-10) and closed it with a repeated call to loving our neighbor (13:8-10). Moreover, he exhorted believers to bless their persecutors, respond nonviolently to evil, and seek peace with all.

By contrast, the state is called to implement justice. Governments stand accountable to God for supporting the good and punishing the evil. The state must address expressions of evil such as terrorism and torture.

Therefore, we distinguish between the role of church and the role of the state.

10. Support and Challenge the State

Followers of Christ should submit to their government, pray for their government (1 Timothy 2:1-4) and support their government's struggle against various manifestations of evil. But exactly how this finds expression varies according to a person's conscience, especially when it comes to "war." Some of us embrace pacifism, others just-war theory and still others just peacemaking.

Followers of Christ also play a prophetic role toward the government. Scripture affirms cases of civil disobedience by God's people (Exodus 1:15-20; Daniel 3:9-18; 6:6-10). The most obvious case was when the apostles boldly affirmed before the religious authorities, "We must obey God rather than men" (Acts 5:29 NASB).

Therefore, we pray for our government and engage politically in accordance with our conscience. We also speak out against governmental policies and practices that we believe are unjust toward Muslims.

CONCLUSION

These ten affirmations describe how we can be agents of peace in a polarized world. They describe what it means for Peace Catalyst International to truly love Muslims and faithfully bear witness to Christ.

Questions

What are the strengths and/or weaknesses of these affirmations?

____

____

Which of these affirmations are most relevant or important to you?

____

____

Which of these affirmations are most easily ignored or forgotten by Christ's followers?

____

____

Take some time to reflect on one or two things you can do to apply these affirmations in your life.

____

____

APPENDIX E

THE JUST-PEACEMAKING PARADIGM

This appendix is from the Just Peacemaking Initiative at Fuller Theological Seminary, http://justpeacemaking.org/the-practices. Used with permission.[1]

The two standard ethical paradigms for the ethics of peace and war are pacifism and just war theory. Both intend to prevent some wars or all wars, but neither focuses our attention on *how* to prevent wars. They focus on debating whether war is justified or not. We believe debates between pacifism and just war theory, while needed, are insufficient. Debates need to focus not only on whether to bomb, whether to make a war, but on what initiatives should be taken to avoid war and spread peace. For that, we need a third paradigm in the debate looking to address the question: "What realistically is working to prevent real wars?" As Glen Stassen and David Gushee articulate in their textbook, *Kingdom Ethics* (InterVarsity Press, 2003):

> If just peacemaking fails, is it right to make war, or should we be committed to nonviolence? Everyone needs an answer to that question, because, short of the second coming, just peacemaking will not prevent all wars. And when war does come, we need to be solidly either just war theorists or pacifists. Otherwise we will be blown about by every wind of ideological interest (Eph 4:14).
>
> Therefore, we urge you not to say, "I support just peacemaking

> theory. It is better than both pacifism and just war theory, and I support it and not them." We do urge you to support just peacemaking theory for what it actually contributes, and to teach it in your church and to demand its practices of your government. We urge you to discuss both pacifism and just war theory carefully, in your Christian community, and seek in prayer and community to discern which is your calling. Then when all else fails, and the government is about to declare war, you can make a clear witness. (p. 174)

We see ten key practices of peacemaking that have been developing ever since World War II working effectively here and there to eliminate potential wars, and to halt terrorism.

PART ONE: PEACEMAKING INITIATIVES

1. Support nonviolent direct action.

Biblical basis: Matt. 5:38-42—Turn the other cheek, give tunic and cloak, go the second mile, give to beggar and borrower; Jesus' way of transforming initiatives

Nonviolent direct action is spreading widely, ending dictatorship in the Philippines, ending rule by the Shah in Iran, bringing about nonviolent revolutions in Poland, East Germany, and Central Europe, transforming injustice into democratic change in human rights movements in Guatemala, Argentina, and elsewhere in Latin America, in South Africa. Governments and people have the obligation to make room for and to support nonviolent direct action.

2. Take independent initiatives to reduce threat.

Biblical basis: Matt. 5:38-42—Turn the other cheek, give tunic and cloak, go the second mile, give to beggar and borrower; Jesus' way of transforming initiatives

Independent initiatives have several characteristics in common. They: (1) are independent of the slow process of negotiation; (2) decrease threat perception and distrust but do not leave the initiator weak; (3) are verifiable actions; (4) and carried out at the announced time regardless of the other side's bluster; (5) have their purpose clearly announced in order to to shift toward de-escalation and to invite reciprocation; and (6) come in a series. Initiatives should continue in order to keep inviting reciprocation.

3. Use cooperative conflict resolution.

Biblical basis: Matt. 5:21-26—Go, make peace with your adversary while there is time.

Cooperative conflict resolution (CCR) incorporates practices like: (1) actively partner in developing solutions, not merely passive cooperation; (2) adversaries, listen to each other and experience each other's perspectives, including culture, spirituality, story, history, and emotion; (3) seek long-term solutions which help prevent future conflict; and (4) seek justice as a core component for sustainable peace. A key test of governments' claims to be seeking peace is whether they initiate negotiations or refuse them, and develop imaginative solutions that show they understand their adversary's perspectives and needs.

Examples: (a) President Carter's achieving peace in the Camp David accords between Egypt and Israel; and (b) peaceful resolution of conflicts with Haiti and North Korea by former president Carter. Unfortunately, Carter's resolution of the conflict with North Korea was cancelled at the beginning of the George W. Bush administration, which rescinded the promised delivery of oil for producing electricity so that North Korea would keep their nuclear generation halted. That administration refused to negotiate with North Korea for six years, contrary to the just peacemaking practice of cooperative conflict resolution, and as we see, the result was North Korea's producing several nuclear bombs.

4. Acknowledge responsibility for conflict and injustice and seek repentance and forgiveness.

Biblical basis: Matt. 7:1-5—Do not judge, but take the log out of your own eye.

Until recently, it was widely agreed that nations would not express regret, acknowledge responsibility, or give forgiveness. But finally Germany since World War II, Japan and Korea, Clinton in Africa, the U.S. toward Japanese-Americans during World War II, the South African Truth and Reconciliation Commission, and other actions (described by Donald Shriver in *An Ethic for Enemies* and by Walter Wink in *When the Powers Fall*) are being recognized as a crucial new practice that can heal longstanding bitterness.

PART TWO: WORKING FOR JUSTICE

5. Advance democracy, human rights, and religious liberty.
Biblical basis: Matt. 6:19-34—Do not hoard, but seek God's reign and justice.

Extensive empirical evidence shows that the spreading of democracy and respect for human rights, including religious liberty, is widening the zones of peace. Democracies fought no wars against one another during the entire twentieth century. They had fewer civil wars. And they generally devoted lower shares of their national products to military expenditures, which decreases threats to other countries. Ties of economic interdependence by trade and investment also decrease the incidence of war. Engagement in international organizations like the UN and regional institutions is a clear predictive factor that they will be much less likely to engage in war.

6. Foster just and sustainable economic development.
Biblical basis: Matt. 6:19-34—Seek God's reign and justice.

"Peace is not only an absence of war, violence, and hostility; it is also a state of reconciliation, human flourishing, and natural beauty" (*Just Peacemaking*, 2008, p. 134). Sustainable development occurs where the needs of today are met without threatening the needs of tomorrow—where those who lack adequate material and economic resources gain access, and those who have learn to control resource use and prevent future exhaustion.

PART THREE: FOSTERING LOVE AND COMMUNITY

7. Work with emerging cooperative forces in the international system.

Biblical basis: Matt. 5:43ff.—Love your enemies, pray for your persecutors; be all-inclusive as your Father in heaven is.

Four trends have so altered the conditions and practices of international relations as to make it possible now, where it was not possible before, to form and sustain voluntary associations for peace and other valuable common purposes that are in fact working: (1) the decline in the utility of war; (2) the priority of trade and the economy over war; (3) the strength of international exchanges, communications, transactions, and networks; and (4) the gradual ascendancy of liberal representative democracy and a mixture of welfare-state and laissez-faire market economy. We should act so as to strengthen these trends and the international associations that they make possible.

8. Strengthen the United Nations and international efforts for cooperation and human rights.

Biblical basis: Matt. 5:43ff.—Love your enemies, pray for your persecutors; be all-inclusive as your Father in heaven is.

Acting alone, states cannot solve problems of trade, debt, interest rates; of pollution, ozone depletion, acid rain, depletion of fish stocks, global warming; of migrations and refugees seeking asylum; of military security when weapons rapidly penetrate borders. Therefore, collective action is increasingly necessary. U.S. citizens should press their government to pay its UN dues and to act in ways that strengthen the effectiveness of the United Nations, of regional organizations, and of multilateral peacemaking, peacekeeping, and peace building. They resolve conflicts, monitor, nurture, and even enforce truces. They meet human needs for food, hygiene, medicine, education, and economic interaction. Most wars now happen within states, not between states; therefore, collective action needs to include UN-approved humanitarian intervention in cases like the former Yugoslavia, Haiti, Somalia, and Rwanda "when a state's condition or behavior results in . . . grave and massive violations of human rights."

9. Reduce offensive weapons and weapons trade.

Biblical basis: Matt. 5:38ff.—Do not set yourself in revengeful retaliation by evil means, but engage in good means of nonviolent confrontational initiatives

A key factor in the decrease of war between nations is that weapons have become so destructive that war is not worth the price. Reducing offensive weapons and shifting toward defensive force structures strengthens that equation. Banning chemical and biological weapons, and reducing strategic (long-range) nuclear warheads from 3,500 to 1,000 each, are key steps. Arms imports by developing nations in 1995 dropped to one-quarter of their peak in 1988. But the power of money invested by arms manufacturers in politicians' campaigns is a major obstacle to reductions. The need for movement on this front domestically can be seen in many recent incidents of gun violence.

10. Encourage grassroots peacemaking groups and voluntary associations.

Biblical basis: Matt. 5.1-2, 7:28-29—Jesus taught the Sermon on the Mount to his disciples; Jesus' strategy of organizing disciples.

The existence of a growing worldwide people's movement constitutes one more historical force that makes just peacemaking theory possible. They learn peacemaking practices and press governments to employ these practices; governments should protect such associations in law, and give them accurate information.

RECOMMENDED READING

Cole, Graham A. *God the Peacemaker: How Atonement Brings Shalom.* Downers Grove, IL: InterVarsity Press, 2009.

Dana, Daniel. *Conflict Resolution.* Madison, WI: McGraw-Hill, 2001.

Fisher, Roger, William Ury and Bruce Patton. *Getting to Yes: Negotiating Agreement Without Giving In.* New York: Penguin Books, 1981.

Gushee, David P. *The Sacredness of Human Life: Why an Ancient Biblical Vision Is Key to the World's Future.* Grand Rapids: Eerdmans, 2013.

Henderson, Michael. *Forgiveness: Breaking the Chain of Hate.* Portland, OR: Arnica, 2002.

Katongole, Emmanuel, and Chris Rice. *Reconciling All Things: A Christian Vision for Justice, Peace and Healing.* Downers Grove, IL: InterVarsity Press, 2008.

Mayer, Bernard. *The Dynamics of Conflict Resolution: A Practitioner's Guide.* San Francisco: Jossey-Bass, 2000.

Noll, Douglas E. *Elusive Peace: How Modern Diplomatic Strategies Could Better Resolve World Conflicts.* Amherst, MA: Prometheus Books, 2011.

Plantinga, Cornelius, Jr. *Not the Way It's Supposed to Be: A Breviary of Sin.* Grand Rapids: Eerdmans, 1995.

Ramsbotham, Oliver, Tom Woodhouse and Hugh Miall. *Contemporary Conflict Resolution,* 2nd ed. Cambridge: Polity, 2005.

Sande, Ken. *The Peacemaker: A Biblical Guide to Resolving Personal Conflict.* Grand Rapids: Baker Book House, 1992.

Scott, Susan. *Fierce Conversations: Achieving Success at Work and in Life, One Conversation at a Time.* New York: Berkely Books, 2004.

Smedes, Lewis B. *The Art of Forgiving.* New York: Ballantine Books, 1997.

Stassen, Glen, ed. *Just Peacemaking: Ten Practices for Abolishing War.* Cleveland: The Pilgrim Press, 2004.

Swartley, Willard M. *Covenant of Peace: The Missing Peace in New Testament Theology and Ethics.* Grand Rapids: Eerdmans, 2006.

Tutu, Desmond. *No Future Without Forgiveness.* New York: Doubleday, 2000.

Volf, Miroslav. *Exclusion and Embrace: A Theological Exploration of Identity, Otherness, and Reconciliation.* Nashville: Abingdon, 1996.

Yoder, Perry B. *Shalom: The Bible's Word for Salvation, Justice, and Peace.* Nappanee, IN: Evangel Publishing House

Wink, Walter. *The Powers That Be.* New York: Doubleday, 1998.

Zahnd, Brian. *Unconditional? The Call of Jesus to Radical Forgiveness.* Lake Mary, FL: Charisma House, 2010.

Zehr, Howard. *The Little Book of Restorative Justice.* Intercourse, PA: Good Books, 2002.

ACKNOWLEDGMENTS

Thank you, Jim Mullins and Michael Ly, for helping me birth Peace Catalyst International. You guys are awesome. Your partnership and encouragement in the work of peace helped shape me and this book. A special thanks to the whole Peace Catalyst team as well. You inspire me and encourage me daily.

Thank you, David Shenk, for being a coach and mentor. You embody peace, speak peace and share the gospel of peace. When struggling with issues, I often think: "What would David do?"

Thank you, Carl Medearis, Tim Lewis and Dennis Hardiman. Your friendship and counsel has been life giving and life guiding. I am deeply grateful that you stood with me in this long transition into becoming a peacemaker.

A number of scholars and leaders have influenced my peacemaking theology and practice. The following deserve special recognition: Joseph Cumming, Miroslav Volf, Glen Stassen, Chris Rice, David Gushee, Bob Roberts Jr., Douglas Johnston, Chris Seiple, Eric Patterson and John Hartley. Thank you for your friendship, example, counsel and writing. When I think of you, I feel like the psalmist who said, "The godly people in the land are my true heroes! I take pleasure in them!" (Psalm 16:3 NLT).

Thank you to my Muslim friends and fellow peacemakers who have especially influenced me and this book: Sayyid Syeed, Mahan Mirza, Safi Kaskas, Samir Kreidie, Ahmad Shqeirat, Usama Shami, Abdel Azim El Siddig and Prince Ghazi bin Muhammad of Jordan. Together let's continue to work for the causes and ideas that we have spent many hours talking about over countless cups of coffee and tea.

Thank you, Kaleen, Tessa and Jessica—my beloved, fun and cool daughters. I am proud of the way you love people, value relationships and resolve conflict. Fran, my beloved, wise and beautiful wife, has faithfully stood with me through every conflict—offering wise counsel and loving support all along. She has also helped me grow through conflict (something rare in a spouse). As a family, we have learned together what it means to be peacemakers. I love you.

I dedicate this book to every person who wants to be and live like a true child of God: "Blessed are the peacemakers, for they will be called children of God" (Matthew 5:9).

NOTES

CHAPTER 1: GOT CONFLICT?

[1]It is worth noting that there was a religious dimension to this conflict. Cain's anger was fueled by religion.

[2]See the A Common Word website, www.acommonword.com/.

[3]"2008 Conference: Loving God and Neighbor in Word and Deed," Yale Center for Faith and Culture, www.faith.yale.edu/faith/common-word/2008-conference.

[4]It was my first book on peacemaking, *Peacemaking: Resolving Conflict, Restoring and Building Harmony in Relationships* (Pasadena, CA: William Carey Library, 2000).

CHAPTER 2: WHAT PEACE CATALYSTS BELIEVE

[1]Emmanuel Katongole and Chris Rice, *Reconciling All Things: A Christian Vision for Justice, Peace and Healing* (Downers Grove, IL: InterVarsity Press, 2008), p. 124.

[2]Willard M. Swartley, *Covenant of Peace: The Missing Peace in New Testament Theology and Ethics* (Grand Rapids: Eerdmans, 2006), pp. 208-11.

[3]*Shalom* is much broader in meaning than the English word *peace*, as I will demonstrate in the next section, "The Peace of God."

[4]Miroslav Volf, *Exclusion and Embrace: A Theological Exploration of Identity, Otherness, and Reconciliation* (Nashville: Abingdon Press, 1996), p. 305.

[5]According to Chris Marshall, *shalom* "combines in one concept the meaning of justice and peace." *The Little Book of Biblical Justice* (Intercourse, PA: Good Books, 2005), p. 13.

Perry B. Yoder argues convincingly that shalom is the Bible's word for salvation, justice and peace in his *Shalom: The Bible's Word for Salvation, Justice and Peace* (Nappanee, IN: Evangel Publishing House, 1987).

[6]Nicholas Wolterstorff, *Until Justice and Peace Embrace* (Grand Rapids: Eerdmans, 1987), p. 69. See also Willard M. Swartley, *Covenant of Peace: The Missing Peace in New Testament Theology and Ethics* (Grand Rapids: Eerdmans, 2006), pp. 27-40.

[7]Shalom " is the well-being of a material, physical, historical kind, not idyllic 'pie in the sky' but 'salvation' in the midst of trees and crops and enemies. . . . It is a vision encompassing all reality." Walter Brueggemann, *Living Toward Vision: Biblical Reflections on Shalom* (New York: United Church Press, 1990), pp. 16-17. Brueggemann's whole book on the topic is excellent.

[8]Cornelius Plantinga Jr., *Not the Way It's Supposed to Be: A Breviary of Sin* (Grand Rapids: Eerdmans), Kindle, p. 10.

[9]See Christopher J. H. Wright, *The Mission of God's People* (Grand Rapids: Zondervan, 2010), pp. 222-43, for a profound description of what it means to live and serve in the public square.

[10]Urbanization is one of the defining traits of the modern world. There are twenty-seven megacities in the world today, with populations over ten million people. There are more than four hundred cities with populations over a million. "The 21st Century will be the first urban century in history. This fact will affect every area of life, and mold the shape of Christian ministries in the future." Patrick Johnstone, *The Future of the Global Church* (Downers Grove, IL: InterVarsity Press, 2011), p. 6. Cities need to be our priority. For an excellent book on the topic, see Eric Swanson and Sam Williams, *To Transform a City* (Grand Rapids: Zondervan, 2010).

[11]"Cities and the Environment," in *World Resources 1996-97: The Urban Environment,* World Resources Institute, www.wri.org/sites/default/files/pdf/worldresources1996-97_bw.pdf.

[12]Why do we see examples of shalom (albeit imperfect) all around us? Because of God's common grace. See "Common Grace, Common Ground, and the Common Good," Peace Catalyst International, part 1, http://peace-catalyst.net/blog/post/common-grace--common-ground--and-the-common-good--part-1-, and part 2, http://peace-catalyst.net/blog/post/common-grace--common-ground--and-the-common-good--part-2-.

[13]"'But as for you, Bethlehem Ephrathah, / Too little to be among the clans of Judah, / From you One will go forth for Me to be ruler in Israel. / His goings forth are from long ago, / From the days of eternity.' / Therefore He will give them up until the time / When she who is in labor has borne a child. / Then the remainder of His brethren / Will return to the sons of Israel. / And He

will arise and shepherd His flock / In the strength of the LORD, / In the majesty of the name of the LORD His God. / And they will remain, / Because at that time He will be great / To the ends of the earth. / This One will be our peace" (Micah 5:2-5 NASB).

"Rejoice greatly, O daughter of Zion! / Shout in triumph, O daughter of Jerusalem! / Behold, your king is coming to you; He is just and endowed with salvation, / Humble, and mounted on a donkey, / Even on a colt, the foal of a donkey. / I will cut off the chariot from Ephraim / And the horse from Jerusalem; / And the bow of war will be cut off. / And He will speak peace to the nations" (Zechariah 9:9-10 NASB).

[14]Many evangelicals understand this prophecy as referring to the new covenant, whereas dispensationalists see this as referring to the millennial age. Even if we understand this from a dispensational perspective, it is still clear that God's long-term game plan is peace. See Willard M. Swartley's magisterial book *Covenant of Peace: The Missing Peace in New Testament Theology and Ethics* (Grand Rapids: Eerdmans, 2006), which was named after this prophecy in Ezekiel.

[15]Christopher J. H. Wright, *The Mission of God's People* (Grand Rapids: Zondervan, 2010), p. 183.

[16]See the four-part series on the Peace Catalyst International website on the holistic nature of the gospel for more background information, beginning with part 1: "Biblical Holism: Is the Good News Just about Getting People into Heaven?" http://peace-catalyst.net/blog/post/biblical-holism:-is-the-good-news-just-about-getting-people-to-heaven.

[17]N. T. Wright, *Simply Jesus* (New York: HarperOne, 2011), p. 218. See also Wright's book *Surprised by Hope: Rethinking Heaven, the Resurrection, and the Mission of the Church* (New York: HarperOne, 2008). He argues that the promise of the future kingdom should inform and guide our present ministry.

[18]Special thanks to Ian Calo for the explanation of this feast.

[19]See Graham Cole, *God the Peacemaker: How Atonement Brings Shalom* (Downers Grove, IL: InterVarsity Press, 2009) for an excellent overview of God's comprehensive peacemaking purposes.

[20]"The Rabbinic attitude towards women was very different from our own. No amount of apologetics can get over the implications of the daily blessing, which Orthodox Judaism has . . . [not removed] from its official prayer book: 'Blessed art thou, O Lord our God, who hast not made me a woman.'" C. G. Montefiore and H. Loewe, *A Rabbinic Anthology* (New York: Schocken

Books, 1974), p. 507. For a more thorough documentation of this, see R. N. Longenecker, *Galatians*, vol. 41, *Word Biblical Commentary*, (1998, electronic ed., Logos Library System), section 156; Scot McKnight, "Original Meaning," in *New Testament: Galatians, NIV Application Commentary* (Grand Rapids: Zondervan, 1995), p. 195.

[21]For the most robust, comprehensive and up-to-date biblical study on this topic, see David P. Gushee, *The Sacredness of Human Life: Why an Ancient Biblical Vision Is Key to the World's Future* (Grand Rapids: Eerdmans, 2013).

[22]Alexander Venter, *Doing Reconciliation: Racism, Reconciliation and Transformation in the Church and World* (Cape Town: Vineyard International Publishing, 2004), p. 179.

[23]The context of Jesus' ministry provides an important insight into the meaning of peacemaking. Jesus lived under Roman rule, ministering in an occupied territory. In the original context of the Beatitudes, this emphasis on peacemaking was most likely directed against the Zealots, Jewish revolutionaries who hoped to throw off the yoke of Roman oppression and to establish the kingdom of God through violence. In contrast to the Zealots, Jesus speaks of a peaceable kingdom and a nonviolent extension of that kingdom.

[24]Glen Stassen, professor of ethics at Fuller Theological Seminary, considers the Sermon on the Mount "the *locus classicus* for Christian peacemaking." *Just Peacemaking: Transforming Initiatives for Justice and Peace* (Louisville, KY: Westminster/John Knox Press, 1992), p. 37.

[25]The Scholars Version of Matthew 5:39 reads, "Don't react violently against the one who is evil." See Glen H. Stassen and David P. Gushee, *Kingdom Ethics: Following Jesus in Contemporary Context* (Downers Grove, IL: Inter-Varsity Press, 2003), pp. 137-40; Walter Wink, *Jesus and Nonviolence* (Minneapolis: Augsburg Fortress, 2003), pp. 98-101; and Swartley, *Covenant of Peace*, 2006, pp. 60-62, for the exegetical basis of this translation.

[26]Dennis E. Johnson's reflections on peacemaking help clarify some of these important principles. See the appendix in John M. Frame, *Evangelical Reunion: Denominations and the Body of Christ* (Grand Rapids: Baker Books, 1991), pp. 170-74.

[27]The concept of discerning and working with a man or woman of peace is a well-recognized missiological principle. People of peace become bridges to reach others because they respond to the gospel or because they at least support those sharing the gospel. What is not a well-recognized missio-

logical principle is the spiritual dynamic of discerning the person of peace by imparting or withdrawing peace.

[28]I am well acquainted with the painful consequences that can ensue because of the gospel. I have had friends who were renounced by their families because they were followers of Christ. I have had friends and acquaintances who were imprisoned and even martyred for the gospel. And I realize that the greatest peacemaker who ever lived was crucified.

[29]It is worth commenting on a few other texts regarding Jesus and the sword. In Luke 22:36-38, Jesus said, "But now if you have a purse, take it, and also a bag; and if you don't have a sword, sell your cloak and buy one. It is written: 'And he was numbered with the transgressors'; and I tell you that this must be fulfilled in me. Yes, what is written about me is reaching its fulfillment." The disciples said, "See, Lord, here are two swords." "That is enough," he replied. Some people interpret this as indicating that Jesus affirmed violence and that he wanted his disciples to use the sword. However, when they drew their swords to protect Jesus during his betrayal, he stopped them immediately: "Put your sword back in its place . . . for all who draw the sword will die by the sword" (Matthew 26:52). And as Jesus stood before Pilate, he said, "My kingdom is not of this world. If it were, my servants would fight to prevent my arrest by the Jewish leaders. But now my kingdom is from another place" (John 18:36). Jesus modeled and proclaimed a kingdom that was extended nonviolently, through love and persuasion, not the sword.

[30]W. C. Kaiser, Peter H. Davids, F. F. Bruce and Manfred T. Brauch, *Hard Sayings of the Bible* (Downers Grove, IL: InterVarsity Press, 1996), p. 378.

[31]Jan Hoeberichts, *Francis and Islam* (Quincy, IL: Franciscan Press, 1997)., p. 5.

[32]I have summarized this event with some quotes from the following works: Mark Galli, *Francis of Assisi and His World* (Downers Grove, IL: InterVarsity 2002); Ida Glaser, "Crusade Sermons, Francis of Assisi and Martin Luther: What does it mean to 'take up the cross' in the context of Islam" in *Crowther Centre Monographs* (Oxford: Church Mission Society, 2010); and Christine A. Mallouhi, *Waging Peace on Islam* (Downers Grove, IL: InterVarsity Press, 2002).

Ida Glaser makes some important observations about St. Francis's ministry among Muslims: "There is no extant writing from Francis himself describing his visit to Al-Kamil; but there is a chapter (16) 'on traveling among Saracens and other infidels' in the first version of his Rule, produced just 2 years after the visit, in 1221. This represents mature thinking about going among Muslims, probably developed in discussion with other brothers. . . . Indeed the friars, who go, can conduct themselves spiritually among them in two manners. One manner is, that they cause no arguments nor strife, but be subject 'to every human creature for God's sake' (1 Pt 2:13) and confess themselves to be Christians. The other manner is, that, when they have seen that it pleases God, they announce the word of God, so that they may believe in God the Omnipotent, Father and Son and Holy Spirit. . . . They are not to cause arguments, but neither are they to hide their Christian faith. They are to be subject to the rulers in the places where they go: that is, they are to abide by Islamic laws when in Muslim territory. They can then discern the right time to announce the word of God. This is extraordinary in a time when polemic argument was a common means of preaching to non-Christians. . . . The crucial question, in which Francis differs most radically from the Crusade sermons, is who are we to love: an aspect of the cross that shines through Francis' writings is *love for enemies*. In contrast, Crusading was based on love for God and love for neighbor, but not on love for enemies. . . . Francis, as we have seen, kept his focus on God's love of enemy as well as friend, and recognized the priority of mission over warfare. For him, God's enemies were not the Muslims over against the Christians, but every sinner which included himself" ("Crusade Sermons," pp. 14-16, 24, 31, emphasis added).

[33]Glaser, *Crusade Sermons*, p. 14.

CHAPTER 3: WHAT PEACE CATALYSTS DO—PART ONE

[1]The Greek term for peace in the New Testament, *eirene,* is defined as "a state of concord, peace, harmony." Walter Bauer et al., *A Greek-English Lexicon of the New Testament and Other Early Christian Literature*, 2nd ed., electronic version.

[2]The apostle Paul addresses these challenges in detail in Romans 14. According to him, faith instructs our own conscience, while love respects the conscience of others. We need to develop God-centered convictions and grace-oriented relations.

[3]It would take a whole book to unpack the profound and practical implications of this quote. The best illustration of this in John Stott's excellent book *Evangelical Truth: A Personal Plea for Unity, Integrity and Faithfulness* (Downers Grove, IL: InterVarsity Press, 1999), esp. pp. 140-44.

[4]Bernard Mayer first introduced me to these three dimensions of conflict resolution. See his *The Dynamics of Conflict Resolution: A Practitioner's Guide*

(San Francisco: Jossey-Bass, 2000), pp. 4-8, 231, 243.

[5]See Howard Zehr, "Restorative Justice" in *Peacebuilding: A Field Guide,* ed. Luc Reychler and Thania Paffenholz (Boulder, CO: Lynne Rienner Publishers, 2001), pp. 330-35, for an excellent, authoritative book on the topic. For further study, see also Restorative Justice Online, www.restorative justice.org.

[6]Desmond Tutu, *No Future Without Forgiveness* (New York: Doubleday, 2000), p. 30.

[7]Ibid., p. 54.

[8]Table adapted from Howard Zehr, *The Little Book of Restorative Justice* (Intercourse, PA: Good Books, 2002), p. 21.

[9]Katy Hutchison, "How a Restorative Response to Crime Changed My Perception of Real Justice," Huffington Post Healthy Living, August 23, 2010, www.huffingtonpost.com/new-harbinger-publications-inc/post_698_b_685505.html.

[10]See Chris Marshall, *The Little Book of Biblical Justice* (Intercourse, PA: Good Books. 2005), pp. 22-48. Marshall notes, "Paul's teaching on the justice of God, especially as it emerges in his letter to the Romans, indicates that he understands divine justice in restorative more than retributive terms" in his *Beyond Retribution: A New Testament Vision for Justice, Crime, and Punishment* (Grand Rapids: Eerdmans. 2001), pp. xiv-xv.

[11]Marshall, *Little Book of Biblical Justice*, p. 48.

[12]Zehr, *Little Book of Restorative Justice*, p. 4.

[13]See Kay Pranis, *The Little Book of Circle Processes: A New/Old Approach to Peacemaking* (Intercourse, PA: Good Books, 2005), p. 9; and Molly Rowan Leach, "Restorative Justice Is on the Rise," Huffington Post Crime, July 23, 2013, www.huffingtonpost.com/molly-rowan-leach/restorative-justice-is-on_b_3612022.html. In 1999 more than three hundred prisons throughout the United States implemented restorative justice programs. David Van Biema, "Should All Be Forgiven?," *TIME Magazine*, March 28, 1999, www.time.com/time/magazine/article/0,9171,22227,00.html.

[14]"Pray for the peace [shalom] of Jerusalem: 'May those who love you be secure. May there be peace [shalom] within your walls and security within your citadels.' For the sake of my family and friends, I will say, 'Peace [shalom] be within you'" (Psalm 122:6-8 NIV; see also Psalm 125:5; 128:6).

[15]The concept of spiritual warfare is most vividly described by Paul the apostle in Ephesians 6:12: "For our struggle is not against flesh and blood, but

against the rulers, against the authorities, against the powers of this dark world and against the spiritual forces of evil in the heavenly realms." For most evangelicals, spiritual warfare includes practices such as personal purity, prayer, fasting, exorcism and resisting the devil by quoting Scripture, which are all important components in our fight against Satan. However, we need to understand spiritual warfare in light of the gospel. Jesus' words and work, his death and resurrection are all aspects of spiritual warfare. They are attacks on the kingdom of darkness (1 John 3:8; Matthew 12:28; Acts 10:38; Colossians 2:15; Ephesians 1:20-21). Thus spiritual warfare is joining Jesus in his battle against Satan to establish the kingdom of God.

[16]Gary Chapman and Jennifer Thomas, *The Five Languages of Apology* (Chicago: Northfield Publishing, 2006), pp. 56-64.

CHAPTER 4: WHAT PEACE CATALYSTS DO—PART TWO

[1]These five essential steps can also be described as the five core competencies of conflict resolution. *Competency* refers to the knowledge and skills necessary to resolve conflict. To describe them as "core" competencies means they are at the heart of all peacemaking.

[2]For more information or to see a summary of Stassen's excellent just-peacemaking practices, see appendix E or visit http://justpeacemaking.org/the-practices.

[3]Glen Stassen, ed., *Just Peacemaking: Ten Practices for Abolishing War* (Cleveland, OH: The Pilgrim Press, 2004), p. 18.

[4]Ibid., p. 18.

[5]If you want to learn more about asking for forgiveness, see *The Five Languages of Apology* by Gary Chapman and Jennifer Thomas. The five languages of apology reflect a full-orbed biblical understanding of what forgiveness entails rather than just describing people's preferred language. In other words, we should use all five languages when we ask for forgiveness—or at least most of them.

[6]The word *forgive* is used for the first time in the story of Joseph: "Forgive your brothers for the great wrong they did to you" (Genesis 50:17 NLT).

[7]See Genesis 42:24; 43:30; 45:2, 14, 15; 46:29; 50:1, 17.

[8]Brian Zahnd, *Unconditional? The Call of Jesus to Radical Forgiveness* (Lake Mary, FL: Charisma House, 2010), p. 72.

[9]Ibid., p. 71.

[10]A New Testament example: Paul the apostle referred to himself as a prisoner

of Jesus Christ—not as a prisoner of Rome (Romans 1:1; Philemon 1:1).

[11]From an interview with Linda on August 21, 2013. The stabbing took place on April 3, 2007. This story was also covered in the following media outlets: Tiara M. Ellis, "Naked Woman Dives at Car, Stabs 1 in Plano," *Dallas Morning News*, www.ar15.com/archive/topic.html?b=1&f=5&t=563729; Josh Hixson, "Victim of naked stabbing in critical condition at Plano hospital," *Plano Star Courier*, starlocalmedia.com/planocourier/news/victim-of-naked-stabbing-in-critical-condition-at-plano-hospital/article-8aaa17f7-ab31-5ff5-bb7f-712e4892ab8d.html; Diane Jennings, "Woman found not guilty by reason of insanity in Plano stabbing," *Dallas Morning News*, www.wfaa.com/news/local/64532187.html.

[12]Lewis B. Smedes, *The Art of Forgiving* (New York: Ballentine Books, 1997), p. 6; and Lewis B. Smedes, "Keys to Forgiving," *Christianity Today*, December 3, 2001, www.christianitytoday.com/ct/2001/december3/42.73.html.

[13]Ken Sande, *The Peacemaker: A Biblical Guide to Resolving Personal Conflict* (Grand Rapids: Baker Books, 1992), p. 164. For a similar defintion, see Jay E. Adams, *A Theology of Christian Counseling* (Grand Rapids: Zondervan, 1979), p. 222.

[14]In rabbinic discussion, the consensus was that a brother might be forgiven a repeated sin three times; on the fourth, there was no forgiveness. Peter, probably thinking himself big-hearted, volunteered "seven times" in answer to his own question—a larger figure often used, among other things, as a "round number" (see Leviticus 26:21; Deuteronomy 28:25; Psalm 79:12; Proverbs 24:16; Luke 17:4). *The Expositor's Bible Commentary*, "Matthew 6. Forgiveness" (18:21-35) 4.0.2, Pradis CD-ROM.

[15]For more on this important topic, see Michael Henderson, *Forgiveness: Breaking the Chain of Hate* (Portland: Arnica Publishing, 2002), and Desmond Tutu's *No Future Without Forgiveness* (New York: Doubleday, 2000).

[16]Miroslav Volf, *Free of Charge: Giving and Forgiving in a Culture Stripped of Grace* (Grand Rapids: Zondervan, 2005), p. 161.

[17]Tutu, *No Future*, pp. 9-10.

[18]L. Gregory Jones, *Embodying Forgiveness: A Theological Analysis* (Grand Rapids: Eerdmans, 1995), pp. 269-70.

[19]See Smedes's excellent reflections on these issues in his *Art of Forgiving*, pp. 23-36, 157-62.

[20]Leah Coulter, *Rediscovering the Power of Repentance and Forgiveness* (Atlanta: Ampelon Publishing, 2006), pp. 135-36. See also Zahnd, *Unconditional*, pp. 118-22.

[21]Zahnd, *Unconditional*, p. 205.

[22]I have adapted and integrated Ron Kraybill's and the Thomas-Kilmann approach to the five styles of conflict.

[23] I forgot to tell John that *Getting to Yes: Negotiating Agreement Without Giving In* by Roger Fisher, William Ury and Bruce Patton is a great resource for learning the skills of collaboration.

[24]Shauna Ries and Susan Harter use a form of the five conflict styles to prepare people for mediation. See their *In Justice inAccord* (BookLocker.com, 2012), pp. 129-34.

CHAPTER 5: HOW PEACE CATALYSTS LOVE

[1]See Richard B. Hays, *The Moral Vision of the New Testament* (San Francisco: Harper, 1996), pp. 320-24, for the various ways interpreters have engaged in the hermeneutics of evasion. See also Glen H. Stassen and David P. Gushee, *Kingdom Ethics: Following Jesus in Contemporary Context* (Downers Grove, IL: InterVarsity Press, 2003), pp. 128-45, for how to understand and apply this command as a transformative initiative.

[2]L. Gregory Jones, *Embodying Forgiveness: A Theological Analysis* (Grand Rapids: Eerdmans, 1995), p. 265.

[3]*The Amman Message* (Amman, Jordan: The Royal Aal al-Bayt Institute for Islamic Thought, 2008), pp. 16-17, refers to four Sunni schools (*madhāhib*) and four non-Sunni schools.

[4]Islamism is "a fundamentalist Islamic revivalist movement generally characterized by moral conservatism and the literal interpretation of the Koran and the attempt to implement Islamic values in all aspects of life." "Islamism," WordNet, http://wordnetweb.princeton.edu/perl/webwn?s=islamism.

[5]For example, see the Royal Aal al-Bayt Institute for Islamic Thought in Jordan www.aalalbayt.org/en/index.html. See also Mohammad Hashim Kamali, *Freedom of Expression in Islam* (Kuala Lumpur: Berita, 1998); Reza Aslan, *No God but God: The Origins, Evolution, and Future of Islam* (New York: Random House, 2006); and Benazir Bhutto, *Reconciliation: Islam, Democracy and the West* (New York: HarperCollins, 2008).

[6]Stephen Schwartz, *The Other Islam: Sufism and the Road to Global Harmony* (New York: Doubleday, 2008), p. 17.

[7]Colin Chapman, "Christian Responses to Islam, Islamism and 'Islamic Terrorism,'" *Cambridge Papers* 16, no. 2 (2007): 5.

[8]These five categories are taken, with names simplified, from *Jihad and the Islamic Law of War,* The Royal Aal al-Bayt Institute for Islamic Thought (2007), pp. 58-60. It is impossible to get a precise percentage of the various categories, but this chart helps capture visually something of the number of Muslims in each category.

[9]See Westboro's websites www.godhatesislam.com, www.godhatesfags.com, and www.godhatesthemedia.com.

[10]See "Grace and Truth: Toward Christlike Relationships with Muslims: An Exposition," http://storage.cloversites.com/peacecatalystinternational/documents/grace%20and%20truth%20exposition%20for%20website_3.pdf.

[11]See, for example, "Muslims Condemn Terrorist Attacks," Al-Muhajabah's Islamic Pages, www.muhajabah.com/otherscondemn.php.

[12]John Stott's excellent chapter "Loving Our Enemies" in *The Cross of Christ* (Downers Grove, IL: 1986), pp. 295-310, has greatly influenced my thinking on this subject.

[13]First Peter 3:9-11 reflects a similar peacemaking ethic: "Do not repay evil with evil or insult with insult. On the contrary, repay evil with blessing, because to this you were called so that you may inherit a blessing. For, 'Whoever among you would love life and see good days must keep your tongue from evil and your lips from deceitful speech. Turn from evil and do good; seek peace and pursue it.'"

[14]While it can be overstated or misapplied, Martin Luther's doctrine of the two kingdoms captures the sense of Romans 12–13. Luther taught that God rules the world in two ways. He rules the earthly, or left-hand, kingdom through the state, which bears the sword. He rules the heavenly, or right-hand, kingdom through the church, which is governed by the Word (see Ewald M. Plass, *What Luther Says*, vol. 1 [St. Louis: Concordia, 1972], pp. 292-96).

[15]"4. Pacifism" in "War," Stanford Encyclopedia of Philosophy, http://plato.stanford.edu/entries/war/#4.

[16]"2. Just War Theory" in "War," Stanford Encyclopedia of Philosophy, http://plato.stanford.edu/entries/war/#2.

[17]I am an enthusiastic supporter of just peacemaking because of its proactive stance toward peace, as I think it best represents what Jesus taught. See Glen Stassen, ed., *Just Peacemaking: Ten Practices for Abolishing War* (Cleveland: Pilgrim Press, 2004), and "The Just Peacemaking Paradigm," Just Peace-

making Initiative, http://justpeacemaking.org/the-practices/.

[18]"An Evangelical Declaration Against Torture: Protecting Human Rights in an Age of Terror, Evangelicals for Human Rights," http://sourcewatch.org/index.php?title=Evangelicals_for_Human_Rights; The New Evangelical Partnership for the Common Good, http://newevangelicalpartnership.org/.

[19]"Public Policy," National Association of Evangelicals, www.nae.net/government-relations/endorsed-documents/409-an-evangelical-declaration-against-torture-protecting-human-rights-in-an-age-of-terror.

[20]Ibid., "7. Concluding Recommendations."

CHAPTER 6: HOW PEACE CATALYSTS MEDIATE AND COMMUNICATE

[1]See Mary Greenwood, *How to Mediate Like a Pro: 42 Rules for Mediating Disputes* (New York: iUniverse, 2008), ix, xi.

[2]Mayer points out that conflict consists of cognitive, emotional and behavioral dimensions. Thus conflict resolution must address all three dimensions. Bernard Mayer, *The Dynamics of Conflict Resolution: A Practitioner's Guide* (San Francisco: Jossey-Bass, 2000), pp. 4-8.

[3]Daniel Dana, *Conflict Resolution* (Madison, WI: McGraw-Hill, 2001), p. 71.

[4]Ibid.

[5]Mayer, *Dynamics of Conflict*, p. 139.

[6]Shauna Ries and Susan Harter, *In Justice inAccord* (BookLocker.com, 2012), p. 117.

[7]There are five conflict styles according to conflict theory: avoidance, competition, compromise, accommodation and collaboration. The goal is to help people work collaboratively to attain peace.

[8]David W. Augsburger, *Conflict Mediation Across Cultures: Pathways and Patterns* (Louisville: Westminster/John Knox Press, 1992), p. 191.

[9]Ken Sande, *The Peacemaker: A Biblical Guide to Resolving Personal Conflict* (Grand Rapids: Baker Books, 1992), p. 127.

[10]See John L. Esposito and Ihsan Yilmaz, eds., *Islam and Peacebuilding: Gülen Movement Initiatives* (New York: Blue Dome Press, 2010), p. 86.

[11]Miroslav Volf describes this as "double vision" in his *Exclusion and Embrace: A Theological Exploration of Identity, Otherness, and Reconciliation* (Nashville: Abingdon Press, 1996), pp. 213-14.

[12]Douglas E. Noll, *Elusive Peace: How Modern Diplomatic Strategies Could Better Resolve World Conflicts* (Amherst, NY: Prometheus Books, 2011), pp. 80, 101.

[13]For information on the conference, go to www.yale.edu/divinity/notes/110705/hope.shtml.

CHAPTER 7: HOW PEACE CATALYSTS WORK ON TEAMS AND IN ORGANIZATIONS

[1]See “Conflict Management Toolbox,” Mediation Training Institute International, www.mediationworks.com/dmi/toolbox.htm.

[2]I originally heard about these four stages from a leader in Youth with a Mission (YWAM). I published an article about it in the *Evangelical Missions Quarterly* (July 1996, pp. 312-16).

[3]See “Following Jesus in a Glocalized World” (paper presented at the Society of Vineyard Scholars, February 3–5, 2011, Seattle), http://ricklove.net/wp-content/uploads/2011/03/Following-Jesus-in-a-Glocalized-World-Rick-Love-2.pdf.

[4]Three books of the best introductory resources available on cultural intelligence are *The Cultural Intelligence Difference* by David Livermore; *Ministering Cross-Culturally: An Incarnational Model for Personal Relationships* by Sherwood G. Lingenfelter and Marvin K. Mayers; and *Cross-Cultural Conflict: Building Relationships for Effective Ministry* by Duane Elmer.

[5]An MOU can include other things, such as educational requirements and strategy. It can be as short or as long as you want.

[6]This communication process needs to involve direction from the Lord and feedback from the team. Jesus is the head of the church and thus the head of the team. As he guides a team, he will sometimes lead them into new directions. He will expose blind spots and show them new areas to emphasize. He will frequently help the team make explicit what is already implicit in its vision and values. Part of the Lord’s guidance comes through team members giving fresh input to the leader. The vision and values must continually be sharpened and refined.

[7]There are a number of excellent resources about personalities and team dynamics. The two I have found most helpful to me personally are the Myers-Briggs Type Indicator (www.myersbriggs.org) and Strength Finders (www.gallupstrengthscenter.com/?gclid=COyfo83727QCFYp_QgodeWAAsQ). Also consider DISC (www.thediscpersonalitytest.com/), the Enneagram (www.enneagraminstitute.com) and PRO-D (www.bluesagestrategies.com).

[8]Patrick Lencioni helped shaped my thinking about these issues. For an

excellent summary, see his *The Advantage: Why Organizational Health Trumps Everything Else in Business* (San Francisco: Jossey-Bass, 2012), pp. 42-47.

CHAPTER 8: HOW PEACE CATALYSTS SPREAD THE PEACE—PART ONE

[1]"'A Common Word' Christian Response," Yale Center for Faith and Culture, www.faith.yale.edu/common-word-christian-response.

[2]Bradley R. E. Wright, *Christians Are Hate-Filled Hypocrites . . . and Other Lies You've Been Told* (Minneapolis: Bethany House, 2010), pp. 155-79.

[3]"Peacemaking Seminar," Peace Catalyst International, www.peace-catalyst.net/training/peacemaking-seminar.

[4]"Love Your Neighbor Dinner," Peace Catalyst International, www.peace-catalyst.net/programs/love-your-neighbor-dinner.

[5]See appendix D, "The Grace and Truth Affirmation," for more about Peace Catalyst's approach to Christian-Muslim relations.

[6]David Kinnaman and Gabe Lyons, *UnChristian: What a New Generation Really Thinks About Christianity . . . and Why It Matters* (Grand Rapids: Baker Books, 2007), p. 3.

[7]I found Andrew Marin's book *Love Is an Orientation: Elevating the Conversation with the Gay Community* (Downers Grove, IL: InterVarsity Press, 2009) very helpful.

[8]Brian Zahnd, *Unconditional? The Call of Jesus to Radical Forgiveness* (Lake Mary, FL: Charisma House, 2010), p. 146.

[9]A quick review of the acts of the flesh reveals our blind spots. Paul lists a number of sins evangelicals ignore to their own peril: "The acts of the sinful nature are obvious: sexual immorality, impurity and debauchery; idolatry and witchcraft; hatred, discord, jealousy, fits of rage, selfish ambition, dissensions, factions and envy; drunkenness, orgies, and the like. I warn you, as I did before, that those who live like this will not inherit the kingdom of God" (Galatians 5:19-21).

[10]I first heard this from my friend Carl Medearis, but I think it first came from Tony Campolo.

[11]This summary uses some direct quotes from Eliza Griswold, "God's Country," *The Atlantic*, March 2008, pp. 40-55. The same story is found in "Warriors and Brothers" in *Peacemakers in Action*, ed. David Little (Cambridge: Cambridge University Press, 2007), and Eliza Griswold, *The Tenth Parallel* (New York: Farrar, Straus and Giroux, 2010).

[12]"Strongest among men in enmity to the Believers will you find the Jews and Pagans; and nearest among them in love to the Believers will you find those who say, 'We are Christians'" (Qur'an 5:82).

[13]"7 Resolutions," Peace Catalyst International, http://peace-catalyst.net/initiatives/7-resolutions.

[14]The Amman Message, www.ammanmessage.com.

CHAPTER 9: HOW PEACE CATALYSTS SPREAD THE PEACE—PART TWO

[1]Our walk with God is not this neat and sequential. We stumble and fall; we get up and are renewed. So God's work of peacemaking can also be compared to a cycle: we continually come back to peace with God, peace with self, peace in the church and so on.

[2]For information on the summit, go to "Evangelicals for Peace," Peace Catalyst, http://peace-catalyst.net/evangelicals-for-peace.

[3]An excellent book on urban peace is Eric Swanson and Sam Williams's *To Transform a City* (Grand Rapids: Zondervan, 2010).

[4]Why does this model of peacemaking favor cities over villages? First, because the Bible provides a model for urban ministry in a way it doesn't for villages. Second, cities are characterized by large populations, diversity and complexity not found in villages. Thus the practices of interpersonal and social peacemaking work well in a village but they are not comprehensive enough for a city. Finally, the practices involved in seeking the shalom of the city can easily apply to life in the village on a simpler scale.

[5]I find Oliver Ramsbotham's three-track approach to diplomacy the most practical. See Oliver Ramsbotham, Tom Woodhouse and Hugh Miall, *Contemporary Conflict Resolution,* 2nd ed. (Cambridge: Polity Press, 2005), pp. 24-26.

[6]According to Kofi Annan, "Over the last two decades more wars have ended through mediation than in the previous two centuries." Isak Svensson and Peter Wallensteen, *The Go-Between* (Washington, DC: United States Institute of Peace Press, 2010), p. ix.

[7]"2008 Conference: Loving God and Neighbor in Word and Deed," Yale Center for Faith and Culture, www.faith.yale.edu/common-word/2008-conference.

[8]"In 1989 alone, thirteen nations comprising 1.7 billion people—over thirty-two percent of humanity—experienced nonviolent revolutions. They suc-

ceeded beyond anyone's wildest expectations in every case but China. And they were completely peaceful (on the part of the protesters) in every case but Romania and parts of the southern U.S.S.R. If we add all the countries touched by major nonviolent actions in this century, the figure reaches almost 3 billion—a staggering sixty-four percent of humanity!" Walter Wink, *The Powers That Be* (New York: Doubleday, 1998), pp. 116-17. For the most detailed account of these peace breakthroughs, see Peter Ackerman and Jack DuVall, *A Force More Powerful: A Century of Nonviolent Conflict* (New York: Palgrave, 2000). Also view *A Force More Powerful,* directed by Steven York (A Force More Powerful Films, 2000), DVD.

[9]Hizbullah means "party of God." This is not the same organization as the Shiite Hezbollah in the Middle East.

[10]This is a summary with some direct quotes taken from David Shenk, "The Gospel of Reconciliation within the Wrath of the Nations," *International Bulletin of Missionary Research* 32, no. 1 (2008): 3-9.

[11]See Susan Scott's brilliant book *Fierce Conversations: Achieving Success at Work and in Life, One Conversation at a Time* (New York: Berkley Books, 2004).

APPENDIX A: IDEAS FOR JOINING GOD IN HIS PEACE MISSION

[1]See my blog on seeking the peace of the city for a simple introduction to the issues: http://peace-catalyst.net/blog/post/incarnational-churches:-seeking-the-peace-of-the-city.

APPENDIX B: SEVEN STEPS TO LOVING REPROOF

[1]Susan Scott's excellent book *Fierce Conversations* (Berkley Books, 2004) helped me make these steps more explicit—though I differ slightly with her at points.

APPENDIX D: THE GRACE AND TRUTH AFFIRMATION

[1]Globalization radically defines and shapes life in the twenty-first century. One important new way of describing globalization is the term *glocalization,* which combines the words *global* and *local* to highlight the comprehensive connectedness of the world in which we live. What happens among the nations impacts our neighbors, and what happens among our neighbors impacts the nations.

[2]See "Subjection to God and Subjection to the State, Part 4," desiringGod, www.desiringgod.org/resource-library/sermons/subjection-to-god-and-subjection-to-the-state-part-4.

APPENDIX E: THE JUST-PEACEMAKING PARADIGM

[1]Fuller Theological Seminary, 135 N Oakland Ave, Pasadena, CA 91182.